Save YOUR Home

From

Probate

In California

First printing, 2022.

Front Page Publishing, LLC

5198 Arlington Ave., Suite 335

Riverside, CA 92504

www.frontpagepublishing.com

Disclaimer

This book is for EDUCATIONAL PURPOSES ONLY!

Seek the advice of an Attorney before using any aspects of this book.

California

Table of Contents

Means of Transferring Real Property Upon Death

The Most Common Means of Transferring Real Property upon Death

The most common means of transferring real property upon death of the owner are three well-known methods: (1) holding property in joint tenancy or as community property with right of survivorship, (2) a living trust, or (3) a will. However, in 2016, a lesser-known alternative to keep a decedent's home out of probate became available to Californians: the revocable transfer on death or "TOD" deed, a simple and inexpensive way to transfer real property to a beneficiary in California.

Including California, TOD deeds are now permitted in 31 states and the District of Columbia. The TOD deed allows a person to leave his or her real property to a designated person or persons such as a family member, friend, life-long partner or other loved one without having to set up a living trust. The TOD deed is considered a nonprobate transfer under Division 5 of the California Probate Code.

Limiting Criteria for Transfer on Death Deed (TOD Deed)

While a TOD deed is attractive because of its simplicity and inexpensiveness, there are specific limiting criteria and procedural requirements for TOD deeds. First and foremost, there are limitations on the type of property that can be transferred through this deed. Only the following are covered:

1. A single-family home or condominium unit,
2. A single-family residence on agricultural property of 40 acres or less, or
3. A residence with no more than four residential dwelling units.

Other requirements are that a revocable TOD deed must be signed and dated before a notary public to be effective and valid; a TOD deed must be recorded within 60 days or less from the date it is signed; and, as its name indicates, the revocable TOD deed can be revoked by the transferor at any time. Upon death of the transferor, the beneficiary must file a Change in

Ownership Statement with the county assessor within 150 days of date of death in accord with Revenue and Taxation Code section 480(b).

It is important to note that the TOD deed must be substantially in the form provided at Probate Code Section 5642, a copy of which follows this article.

Revoking a Transfer on Death Deed

The transferor or owner can revoke a TOD deed in any of three ways: (1) the owner can record a formal notice of revocation; (2) a new TOD deed may be recorded; or (3) the real property can be transferred to someone else prior to the transferor's death.

Effect of Recording a TOD Deed

Although the transfer on death deed must be recorded within 60 days or less from the date it is it signed and before the owner's death, the interest in the real estate only transfers when the owner dies. Accordingly, the beneficiary identified on the TOD deed does not have any rights to the real property when the owner is alive. Furthermore, creditors of a named beneficiary cannot place any liens on the property. Of course, while the owner is living, the owner has the right to sell or encumber the property and it is also subject to involuntary liens that may be recorded by creditors of the owner which would transfer with the property to the beneficiary upon the owner's death.

TOD Deeds, Joint Tenancy, and Community Property

A TOD deed may not be ideal for use with property held in joint tenancy or owned as community property. Pursuant to Probate Code section 5664, if title is held in joint tenancy or community property with right of survivorship, then at the time of the transferor's death, the TOD deed is void if the other spouse, registered domestic partner, or joint tenant is still alive. Under those circumstances, executing a TOD deed has no effect. However, if the transferor decedent is the last joint tenant or spouse to die, the TOD deed takes effect and controls the ownership of the property upon date of death.

TOD deeds and Creditors' Claims

Real property subject to a TOD deed remains subject to the claims of the transferor's creditors. The beneficiary of a TOD deed is personally liable to the transferor's estate and the transferor's creditors. The personal representative of the transferor's estate may demand restitution from a TOD deed beneficiary. This demand may occur as late as three years after the decedent's death.

Pros & Cons of a Transfer on Death Deed

As with any method of estate planning, there are advantages and disadvantages with TOD deeds. Whether these will balance out in any particular circumstance will differ from person to person and from property to property. Summarized below are some of the more important pros and cons that will affect the decision of whether a TOD deed would be appropriate.

Pros

1. Filing and recording the transfer on death deed is fast, simple, and very inexpensive (especially compared to the living trust and last will options).
2. The TOD deed protects the property from probate as long as the beneficiary does not predecease the grantor.
3. The TOD deed is fully revocable during the real property owner's lifetime.
4. The TOD permits the grantor to retain full ownership of the property during his or her lifetime, instead of adding the beneficiary as a joint tenant and making him or her an immediate legal owner.
5. The recording of a TOD deed is not a taxable event. By contrast, adding a joint tenant is considered a gift by the IRS and requires the filing of a gift tax return, not to mention possible higher taxes in the future.

Cons

1. The property will be subject to probate if the beneficiary predeceases the grantor and there is no alternate estate plan.
2. If property is co-owned in joint tenancy, the surviving joint tenant becomes the sole owner upon the other's death and has full control of the property despite the TOD deed,

unless the co-tenant has also filed a TOD deed separately naming the same beneficiary or beneficiaries.

3. If the beneficiary is a minor upon the death of the property owner, a court-appointed custodian will be granted control and management of the property until the child reaches legal age, and only then will the child own the property outright. This process may incur legal and court fees.
4. If the owner becomes incapacitated through stoke, dementia, or other event, there may be no one to revoke the deed, which may be necessary due to a change in family circumstances or the need to qualify the person for Medicaid assistance.
5. Should the real property owner pass away, the named beneficiary will be held personally liable for all unsecured debts (mortgages and taxes) of the deceased property owner, up to the value of the property that passes to the named beneficiary.
6. The property may still be subject to Medi-Cal estate recovery if the property owner was a recipient of Medi-Cal benefits.

Sunset Date

As stated above, the use of TOD deeds is relatively new, and they are not allowed in all states. In California, we have undertaken a five-year trial period for TOD deeds. According to the California legislation, the use of TOD deeds needs to be re-authorized by the California legislature or approval of the use of TOD deeds will expire on December 31, 2020. In that event, after January 1, 2021, any revocable TOD deed that is properly executed during the five-year period will remain valid until the property owner dies or revokes the deed.

Preparation Of the Transfer on Death Deed

How Do I Prepare the Transfer on Death Deed?

Fortunately, the process of filing and recording the transfer on death deed to leave real estate for a beneficiary is quite simple. The copy of the deed you prepare must meet state requirements and contain the correct language and formatting. This simple, one-page document can be found for free at your county clerk's office or website. Los Angeles County offers the form for free here. These are the simple steps to making sure your transfer on death deed is prepared correctly:

1. Fill out all general required information about your identity and address. Make sure the "Assessor's Parcel Number" and "Property Description" directly matches the description from your property's current deed, or your deed may be invalid if it isn't titled correctly.
2. Name your beneficiary or beneficiaries. Be specific and do not use categories such as "my children" or "my brother." The state will likely not recognize these types of titles even if your identity is clear. It is safest to list the full legal name of each beneficiary you wish to name.
    a. If you name more than one beneficiary, be sure to indicate how they will take title to your property upon your death. Will they be titled "as joint tenants" who will own the property in equal shares?
3. Sign and date the transfer on death deed before a notary public. If you're not the sole owner of your property, then the transfer on death deed is useless if you predecease your co-tenant, who will own the property outright. Your co-tenant (such as a spouse or sibling) would have to file a separate transfer on death deed naming the same beneficiaries in order to ensure the transfer of property in the event of both property owners' deaths.
4. Have the notarized deed recorded with your county clerk's office. Remember that the law requires you to record the deed within 60 days of notarization, otherwise it will be null. This can be done by mailing or bringing your deed to your local recorder/county clerk's office. Be prepared to any filing and recording fees.

How Do I Revoke a Transfer on Death Deed?

The transfer on death deed is fully revocable before the death of the real property owner. There are 3 effective ways to revoke this deed:

1. File and record a Revocation of Revocable Transfer on Death Deed form.
2. Record a new transfer on death deed naming a different beneficiary. The newest recorded deed will automatically revoke any and all previous deeds of the same type.

3. Sell or transfer the real property to someone else prior to the real property owner's death.

Potential Risks and Uncertainties of the Transfer on Death Deed

Since the transfer on death deed was only recently introduced as a legal way to transfer property upon a property owner's death, there are several legal implications that have not been fully studied and understood yet.

There are possible unforeseen or unintended consequences of having the transfer on death deed as a new option for real property transfer:

1. Opponents of the transfer on death deed have cited concerns relating to issues of undue influence, fraud, or incompetence when it comes to preparing these deeds. For example, scammers or predators may persuade or pressure an elderly person to prepare this type of deed to transfer a home to them upon death. Elder abuse and other types of undue influence or fraud are a main concern. The current safeguard for this is a law that prohibits a beneficiary from selling a home within 120 days of the grantor's death.
2. Claims of undue influence, fraud, or incompetence may invite litigation by family members and friends upon the death of a property owner who prepared a transfer on death deed.
3. Any mortgage or debt that is attached to the property is transferred along with the property to the beneficiary upon the property owner's death.
4. Any liens placed upon a property by the homeowner's creditors are transferred to the beneficiary upon the homeowner's death.

What if I'm a Co-Owner of a Property?

There are several ways to own a property jointly, with one or more people such as a spouse, family member, or friends. There is joint tenancy with right of survivorship, community property (with or without right of survivorship), or tenancy in common. Joint tenancy is the main form of co-ownership that may affect the use of a transfer on death deed.

If you co-own a property under joint tenancy, things can get tricky if you want to leave property to a beneficiary with a transfer on death deed. Legally, your joint tenant(s) has the right of survivorship and would inherit your share of the property upon your death. This means that even if you had a transfer on death deed prepared, it becomes useless since your joint tenant now owns the property in full. There are only two ways to avoid your transfer on death deed from becoming null:

1. You outlive the other joint tenant(s).
2. Your joint tenant(s) shares your interests and prepares a separate transfer on death deed naming the same beneficiary. However, since this deed is fully revocable, your joint tenant may choose to revoke the deed upon your death, making your joint tenant the sole owner of the property.

The Transfer on Death Deed In A Nutshell

The transfer on death deed, like any other method of estate planning, has its benefits and drawbacks. These pros and cons all depend on the status of your finances, the amount of assets you possess, the urgency of your situation, and much more. Any type of estate planning is a step in the right direction if you have your loved ones' futures in mind. However, it is always safest to consult with a trusted estate planning attorney if you are ever unsure about your options.

Conclusion

Because of the disadvantages outlined above, particularly concerns regarding joint tenancy, community property, transfers to minors, and capacity to revoke, some estate planners believe that transfer on death deeds should only be used as a last resort if there is insufficient time to prepare proper estate documents. Additionally, this type of deed is not particularly necessary for married couples who can avoid probate by simply owning their home under joint tenancy or community property where, if one spouse dies, the surviving spouse would fully inherit the other's share. But despite these limitations, a revocable transfer upon death deed may be an ideal option for a single person whose only asset is the home in which he or she lives.

Forms

SIMPLE REVOCABLE TRANSFER ON DEATH (TOD) DEED
(California Probate Code Section 5642)

Recording Requested By:

When Recorded Mail This Deed To

Name:

Address:

Assessor's Parcel Number:Space Above For Recorder's Use

This document is exempt from documentary transfer tax under Rev. & Tax. Code § 11930. This document is exempt from preliminary change of ownership report under Rev. & Tax. Code § 480.3.

IMPORTANT NOTICE: THIS DEED MUST BE RECORDED ON OR BEFORE 60 DAYS AFTER THE DATE IT IS SIGNED AND NOTARIZED

Use this deed to transfer the residential property described below directly to your named beneficiaries when you die. YOU SHOULD CAREFULLY READ ALL OF THE INFORMATION ON THE OTHER PAGES OF THIS FORM. You may wish to consult an attorney before using this deed. It may have results that you do not want. Provide only the information asked for in the form. DO NOT INSERT ANY OTHER INFORMATION OR INSTRUCTIONS. This form MUST be RECORDED on or before 60 days after the date it is signed and notarized or it will not be effective.

PROPERTY DESCRIPTION

Print the legal description of the residential property affected by this deed:

BENEFICIARY(IES)

Print the FULL NAME(S) of the person(s) who will receive the property on your death (DO NOT use general terms like "my children") and state the RELATIONSHIP that each named person has to you (spouse, son, daughter, friend, etc.):

TRANSFER ON DEATH

I transfer all of my interest in the described property to the named beneficiary(ies) on my death. I may revoke this deed. When recorded, this deed revokes any TOD deed that I made before signing this deed. Sign and print your name below (your name should exactly match the name shown on your title documents):

Date

NOTE: This deed only transfers MY ownership share of the property. The deed does NOT transfer the share of any co-owner of the property. Any co-owner who wants to name a TOD beneficiary must execute and RECORD a SEPARATE deed.

WITNESSES

To be valid, this deed must be signed by two persons, both present at the same time, who witness your signing of the deed or your acknowledgment that it is your deed. The signatures of the witnesses do not need to be acknowledged by a notary public.

Witness #1
Print and sign your name:

Witness #2
Print and sign your name:

ACKNOWLEDGMENT OF NOTARY

A notary public or other officer completing this certificate verifies only the identity of the individual who signed the document to which this certificate is attached, and not the truthfulness, accuracy, or validity of that document.

State of California)

County of)

On ________________________ before me, (here insert name and title of the officer), personally appeared ________________________, who proved to me on the basis of satisfactory evidence to be the person(s) whose name(s) is/are subscribed to the within instrument and acknowledged to me that he/she/they executed the same in his/her/their authorized capacity(ies), and that by his/her/their signature(s) on the instrument the person(s), or the entity upon behalf of which the person(s) acted, executed the instrument.

I certify under PENALTY OF PERJURY under the laws of the State of California that the foregoing paragraph is true and correct.

WITNESS my hand and official seal.

Signature ________________________ (Seal)

(b) Subsequent pages of a form executed under this section shall be in substantially the following form.

COMMON QUESTIONS ABOUT THE USE OF THIS FORM

WHAT DOES THE TOD DEED DO? When you die, the identified property will transfer to your named beneficiary without probate. The TOD deed has no effect until you die. You can revoke it at any time.

CAN I USE THIS DEED TO TRANSFER BUSINESS PROPERTY? This deed can only be used to transfer (1) a parcel of property that contains one to four residential dwelling units, (2) a condominium unit, or (3) a parcel of agricultural land of 40 acres or less, which contains a single-family residence.

HOW DO I USE THE TOD DEED? Complete this form. Have it notarized. RECORD the form in the county where the property is located. The form MUST be recorded on or before 60 days after the date you sign it or the deed has no effect.

IS THE "LEGAL DESCRIPTION" OF THE PROPERTY NECESSARY? Yes.

HOW DO I FIND THE "LEGAL DESCRIPTION" OF THE PROPERTY? This information may be on the deed you received when you became an owner of the property. This information may also be available in the office of the county recorder for the county where the property is located. If you are not absolutely sure, consult an attorney.

HOW DO I "RECORD" THE FORM? Take the completed and notarized form to the county recorder for the county in which the property is located. Follow the instructions given by the county recorder to make the form part of the official property records.

WHAT IF I SHARE OWNERSHIP OF THE PROPERTY? This form only transfers YOUR share of the property. If a co-owner also wants to name a TOD beneficiary, that co-owner must complete and RECORD a separate form.

CAN I REVOKE THE TOD DEED IF I CHANGE MY MIND? Yes. You may revoke the TOD deed at any time. No one, including your beneficiary, can prevent you from revoking the deed.

HOW DO I REVOKE THE TOD DEED? There are three ways to revoke a recorded TOD deed: (1) Complete, have notarized, and RECORD a revocation form. (2) Create, have notarized, and RECORD a new TOD deed. (3) Sell or give away the property, or transfer it to a trust, before your death and RECORD the deed. A TOD deed can only affect property that you own when you die. A TOD deed cannot be revoked by will.

CAN I REVOKE A TOD DEED BY CREATING A NEW DOCUMENT THAT DISPOSES OF THE PROPERTY (FOR EXAMPLE, BY CREATING A NEW TOD DEED OR BY ASSIGNING THE PROPERTY TO A TRUST)? Yes, but only if the new document is RECORDED. To avoid any doubt, you may wish to RECORD a TOD deed revocation form before creating the new instrument. A TOD deed cannot be revoked by will, or by purporting to leave the subject property to anyone via will.

IF I SELL OR GIVE AWAY THE PROPERTY DESCRIBED IN A TOD DEED, WHAT HAPPENS WHEN I DIE? If the deed or other document used to transfer your property is RECORDED before your death, the TOD deed will have no effect. If the transfer document is not RECORDED before your death, the TOD deed will take effect.

I AM BEING PRESSURED TO COMPLETE THIS FORM. WHAT SHOULD I DO? Do NOT complete this form unless you freely choose to do so. If you are being pressured to dispose of your property in a way that you do not want, you may want to alert a family member, friend, the district attorney, or a senior service agency.

DO I NEED TO TELL MY BENEFICIARY ABOUT THE TOD DEED? No. But secrecy can cause later complications and might make it easier for others to commit fraud.

WHAT DOES MY BENEFICIARY NEED TO DO WHEN I DIE? Your beneficiary must RECORD evidence of your death (Prob. Code § 210), and file a change in ownership notice (Rev. & Tax. Code § 480). If you received Medi-Cal benefits, your beneficiary must notify the State Department of Health Care Services of your death and provide a copy of your death certificate (Prob. Code § 215).

WHAT IF I NAME MORE THAN ONE BENEFICIARY? Your beneficiaries will become co-owners in equal shares as tenants in common. If you want a different result, you should not use this form.

HOW DO I NAME BENEFICIARIES? You MUST name your beneficiaries individually, using each beneficiary's FULL name. You MAY NOT use general terms to describe beneficiaries, such as "my children." For each beneficiary that you name, you should briefly state that person's relationship to you (for example, my spouse, my son, my daughter, my friend, etc.).

WHAT IF A BENEFICIARY DIES BEFORE I DO? If all beneficiaries die before you, the TOD deed has no effect. If a beneficiary dies before you, but other beneficiaries survive you, the share of the deceased beneficiary will be divided equally between the surviving beneficiaries. If that is not the result you want, you should not use the TOD deed.

WHAT IS THE EFFECT OF A TOD DEED ON PROPERTY THAT I OWN AS JOINT TENANCY OR COMMUNITY PROPERTY WITH RIGHT OF SURVIVORSHIP? If you are the first joint tenant or spouse to die, the deed is VOID and has no effect. The property transfers to your joint tenant or surviving spouse and not according to this deed. If you are the last joint tenant or spouse to die, the deed takes effect and controls the ownership of your property when you die. If you do not want these results, do not use this form. The deed does NOT transfer the share of a co-owner of the property. Any co-owner who wants to name a TOD beneficiary must complete and RECORD a SEPARATE deed.

CAN I ADD OTHER CONDITIONS ON THE FORM? No. If you do, your beneficiary may need to go to court to clear title.

IS PROPERTY TRANSFERRED BY THE TOD DEED SUBJECT TO MY DEBTS? Yes.

DOES THE TOD DEED HELP ME TO AVOID GIFT AND ESTATE TAXES? No.

HOW DOES THE TOD DEED AFFECT PROPERTY TAXES? The TOD deed has no effect on your property taxes until your death. At that time, property tax law applies as it would to any other change of ownership.

DOES THE TOD DEED AFFECT MY ELIGIBILITY FOR MEDI-CAL? No.

AFTER MY DEATH, WILL MY HOME BE LIABLE FOR REIMBURSEMENT OF THE STATE FOR MEDI-CAL EXPENDITURES? Your home may be liable for reimbursement. If you have questions, you should consult an attorney.

5644.

A transferor may revoke a revocable transfer on death deed by an instrument in substantially the following form:

Revocation of
Revocable Transfer on Death (TOD) Deed

(California Probate Code Section 5600)

Recording Requested By:

When Recorded Mail This Deed To

Name:

Address:

Assessor's Parcel Number:Space Above For Recorder's Use

This deed revocation is exempt from documentary transfer tax under Rev. & Tax. Code §11930. This deed revocation is exempt from preliminary change of ownership report under Rev. & Tax. Code § 480.3.

IMPORTANT NOTICE: THIS FORM MUST BE RECORDED TO BE EFFECTIVE

This revocation form MUST be RECORDED before your death or it will not be effective. This revocation form only affects a transfer on death deed that YOU made. A transfer on death deed made by a co-owner of your property is not affected by this revocation form. A co-owner who wants to revoke a transfer on death deed that he/she made must complete and RECORD a SEPARATE revocation form.

PROPERTY DESCRIPTION

Print the legal description of the property affected by this revocation:

REVOCATION

I revoke any TOD deed to transfer the described property that I executed before executing this form.

SIGNATURE AND DATE

Sign and print your name below (your name should exactly match the name shown on your title documents):

_______________________________ Date

To be valid, this deed must be signed by two persons, both present at the same time, who witness your signing of the deed or your acknowledgment that it is your deed. The signatures of the witnesses do not need to be acknowledged by a notary public.

Witness #1 Print and sign your name:	Witness #2 Print and sign your name:
_______________	_______________

ACKNOWLEDGMENT OF NOTARY

A notary public or other officer completing this certificate verifies only the identity of the individual who signed the document to which this certificate is attached, and not the truthfulness, accuracy, or validity of that document.

State of California)

County of)

On ________________________ before me, (here insert name and title of the officer), personally appeared ________________________, who proved to me on the basis of satisfactory evidence to be the person(s) whose name(s) is/are subscribed to the within instrument and acknowledged to me that he/she/they executed the same in his/her/their authorized capacity(ies), and that by his/her/their signature(s) on the instrument the person(s), or the entity upon behalf of which the person(s) acted, executed the instrument.

I certify under PENALTY OF PERJURY under the laws of the State of California that the foregoing paragraph is true and correct.

WITNESS my hand and official seal.

Signature ________________________ (Seal)

California Transfer on Death Deed Revocation Form

Recording requested by (name):

____

When recorded mail to
and mail tax statements to:

____

____

____

____

Recorder's Use Only

REVOCATION OF REVOCABLE TRANSFER ON DEATH DEED

(California Probate Code Section 5600)

This document is exempt from documentary transfer tax under Rev. & Tax. Code § 11930. This document is exempt from preliminary change of ownership report under Rev. & Tax. Code § 480.3.

Assessor's Parcel No.:

____

Declaration of Exemption From Gov't Code § 27388.1 Fee

☐ Transfer is exempt from fee per GC § 27388.1(a)(2):
- ☐ recorded concurrently "in connection with" transfer subject to Documentary Transfer Tax
- ☐ recorded concurrently "in connection with" a transfer of residential dwelling to an owner-occupier

☐ Transfer is exempt from fee per GC 27388.1(a)(1):
- ☐ Fee cap of $225.00 reached ☐ Not related to real property

IMPORTANT NOTICE: THIS FORM MUST BE RECORDED TO BE EFFECTIVE

This revocation form MUST be RECORDED before your death or it will not be effective. This revocation form only affects a transfer on death deed that YOU made. A transfer on death deed made by a co-owner of your property is not affected by this revocation form. A co-owner who wants to revoke a transfer on death deed that he/she made must complete and RECORD a SEPARATE revocation form.

PROPERTY DESCRIPTION

Print the legal description of the property affected by this revocation:

____

____

____

REVOCATION

I, ______________________________, am the transferor under the Revocable TOD deed dated ______________ and recorded on ______________ as Instrument No. ______________ in Book/Reel ________, Page/Image ________, of Official Records of ______________________________ County, California, which named as beneficiary(ies) ______________________________

____.

I hereby revoke any TOD deed to transfer the described property that I executed before executing this form, including the TOD deed described above.

SIGNATURE AND DATE

Sign and print your name below (your name should exactly match the name shown on your title documents):

Date: ____________________

____
(Signature of declarant)

____
(Typed or written name of declarant)

ACKNOWLEDGMENT

A Notary Public or other officer completing this certificate verifies only the identity of the individual who signed the document to which this certificate is attached, and not the truthfulness, accuracy, or validity of that document.

State of California)
County of ______________________)

On __________________________ before me, ______________________________________
(insert name and title of the officer)

personally appeared ____
who proved to me on the basis of satisfactory evidence to be the person(s) whose name(s) is/are subscribed to the within instrument and acknowledged to me that he/she/they executed the same in his/her/their authorized capacity(ies), and that by his/her/their signature(s) on the instrument the person(s), or the entity upon behalf of which the person(s) acted, executed the instrument.

I certify under PENALTY OF PERJURY under the laws of the State of California that the foregoing paragraph is true and correct.

WITNESS my hand and official seal. **(Seal)**

Signature ____________________________________

WHAT IS A POWER OF ATTORNEY AND WHY YOU MAY NEED ONE?

CONTENTS

WHAT IS A POWER OF ATTORNEY?

A power of attorney (POA) is a legal document giving one person (the agent or attorney-in-fact) the power to act for another person (the principal). This agent can have broad legal or limited authority to make decisions about the principal's property, finances, or medical care. The power of attorney is frequently used in the event of a principal's illness or disability, or when the principal can't be present to sign necessary documents for financial transactions.

A power of attorney can end for a number of reasons, such as when the principal dies, the principal revokes it, a court invalidates it, the principal divorces their spouse, who happens to be the agent, or the agent can no longer carry out the outlined responsibilities.

Conventional POAs lapse when the creator becomes incapacitated. A “durable” POA remains in force to enable the agent to manage the creator’s affairs, and a “springing” POA comes into effect only if and when the creator of the POA becomes incapacitated. A medical or healthcare POA enables an agent to make medical decisions on behalf of an incapacitated person.

UNDERSTANDING POWER OF ATTORNEY

A power of attorney should be considered when planning for long-term care. There are different types of POAs that fall under either a general power of attorney or limited power of attorney.

A general power of attorney acts on behalf of the principal in any and all matters, as allowed by the state. The agent under a general POA agreement may be authorized to take care of issues such as handling bank accounts, signing checks, selling property and assets like stocks, filing taxes, etc.

A limited power of attorney gives the agent the power to act on behalf of the principal in specific matters or events. For example, the limited POA may explicitly state that the agent is only allowed

to manage the principal's retirement accounts. A limited POA may also be in effect for a specific period of time (e.g., if the principal will be out of the country for, say, two years).
Most powers of attorney documents allow an agent to represent the principal in all property and financial matters as long as the principal's mental state of mind is good. If a situation occurs where the principal becomes incapable of making decisions for themself, the POA agreement would automatically end. However, someone who wants the POA to remain in effect after the person's health deteriorates would need to sign a durable power of attorney (DPOA).

A person appointed as power of attorney is not necessarily an attorney. The person could be a trusted family member, friend, or acquaintance.

UNDERSTANDING THE DURABLE POWER OF ATTORNEY (DPOA)

The durable power of attorney (DPOA) remains in control of certain legal, property, or financial matters specifically spelled out in the agreement, even after the principal becomes mentally incapacitated. While a DPOA can pay medical bills on behalf of the principal, the durable agent cannot make decisions related to the principal's health (e.g., taking the principal off life support is not up to a DPOA).

The principal can sign a durable power of attorney for health care, or healthcare power of attorney (HCPA), if they want an agent to have the power to make health-related decisions. This document also called a healthcare proxy, outlines the principal's consent to give the agent POA privileges in the event of an unfortunate medical condition. The durable POA for healthcare is legally bound to oversee medical care decisions on behalf of the principal.

Another type of DPOA is the durable power of attorney for finances, or simply a financial power of attorney. This document allows an agent to manage the business and financial affairs of the principal, such as signing checks, filing tax returns, mailing and depositing Social Security checks, and managing investment accounts, in the event, the latter becomes unable to understand or make decisions. To the extent of what the agreement spells out as the agent's responsibility, the agent has to carry out the principal's wishes to the best of their ability.

When the agent acts on behalf of the principal by making investment decisions through a broker or medical decisions through a healthcare professional, both institutions would ask to see the DPOA. Although the DPOA for both medical and financial matters can be one document, it is good to have separate DPOAs for healthcare and finances. Since the DPOA for healthcare will have the principal's personal medical information, it would be inappropriate for the broker to have it, and the medical professionals don't need to know the financial status of the patient either.

The conditions for which a durable POA may become active are set up in a document called the springing power of attorney. The springing POA defines the kind of event or level of incapacitation that should occur before the DPOA springs into effect. A power of attorney can remain dormant until a negative health occurrence activates it to a DPOA.

HOW POWER OF ATTORNEY WORKS

You can buy or download a power of attorney template. If you do, be sure it is for your state, as requirements differ. However, this document may be too important to leave to the chance that you got the correct form and handled it properly.

A better way to start the process of establishing a power of attorney is by locating an attorney who specializes in family law in your state. If attorney's fees are more than you can afford, legal services offices staffed with credentialed attorneys exist in virtually every part of the United States. Visit the Legal Services Corporation's website, which has a "Find Legal Aid" search function. Clients who qualify will receive pro bono (cost-free) assistance.[1]

Certain circumstances may trigger the desire for a power of attorney (POA) for someone over the age of 18. For example, someone in the military might create a POA before deploying overseas so that another person can act on their behalf should they become incapacitated.

Incapacity isn't the only reason someone might need a POA, though. Expatriates workers and families need to set a POA for their affairs in America while doing their work overseas. Younger people who travel a great deal might set up a POA so that someone can handle their affairs in their absence, especially if they have no spouse to do so. However, POAs are most commonly established when someone is elderly or if they face a serious, more long-term health crisis.

If you have a POA and become unable to act on your own behalf due to mental or physical incapacity, your agent or attorney-in-fact may be called upon to make financial decisions to ensure your well-being and care. For example, they may need to pay bills, sell assets to pay for medical expenses, and take steps for Medicaid planning for you.

Other important tasks a POA can authorize someone to carry out are banking transactions, real estate decisions, dealing with government or retirement benefits, and healthcare billing.

How to Get a Power of Attorney (POA)

The first thing to do if you want a power of attorney is to select someone you trust to handle your affairs if and when you cannot. Then you must decide what the agent can do on your behalf, and in what circumstances. For example, you could establish a POA that only happens when you are no longer capable of handling your affairs yourself—or one that goes into effect immediately so your agent can act for you In your absence.

Some powers of attorney are limited. For instance, the POA could merely empower someone to represent you at a real estate closing in another city. Also, note that even when a general POA contains no such limiting language, it usually only operates while the person conveying the power, called "the principal," has full capacity.

If you have property that is only in your name, your spouse would need a power of attorney to take legal or financial actions related to that property (like selling it).

Anyone can set up a POA. One way is to find a template online that satisfies the requirements of the state in which you live, and execute it according to your state's guidelines (it may need to be notarized and require witnesses).

POAs differ depending on when you want the authority to start and end, how much responsibility you want to give your agent, and the laws in the state where you live. There is no uniform POA common to every state. States have different requirements for establishing a power of attorney—Pennsylvania's statute, for instance, makes the legal assumption that a power of attorney is durable.

Using an attorney to draw up the POA will help ensure that it conforms with state requirements. Since a POA may be questioned if an agent needs to invoke it with a bank or financial services company, you should ask an attorney about prior experience in drafting such powers. You want to select someone not only familiar with state requirements, but also with the issues that can arise when a power is invoked. This way, the attorney can use language that will make clear the full extent of the responsibilities that you wish to convey.

To set up a legally binding POA, the principal must have sufficient mental capacity when the document is drawn up. This means that they must fully understand the nature and effect of the document. It also means that if you have an ill parent who is already incapacitated, you won't be able to get a power of attorney to act on their behalf.

The POA can be canceled or revoked at any time simply by destroying the original document and preparing a new one, or by preparing a formal revocation document informing all concerned that the POA is no longer a valid instrument.

WHAT HAPPENS IF YOU LACK A POWER OF ATTORNEY (POA)

POAs are not just reassuring; they may become the instruments that protect your financial and real estate interests, your health, and even your manner of dying. If you are incapacitated and have no POA designated to take the wheel, your family will likely be forced into costly and time-consuming delays.

Principals have to set up POAs for themselves. A family can't "get" a POA when they suddenly realize that an elderly relative is no longer able to manage their affairs. In this situation, a court would have to appoint a guardian or conservator, and neither the individual nor their family would have any control over the appointee. In some states, the guardian is required to post a bond and file a detailed inventory and accounting of the person's relevant assets. The entire affair is more complicated, more costly—and more public —when a POA is not already in place.

FOUR TYPES OF POAS

There are several types of POAs, as well as various degrees of responsibility that you can delegate.

Conventional POA

This starts when it is signed and continues in force *until* you become mentally unable to make coherent decisions. It is important to state exactly what authority you are giving your agent. It could be something very specific, like giving your attorney the power to sign a deed of sale for your house while you're on a trip around the world.

This is called a "limited power of attorney" and it can be quite common in everyday life. One common use of it is what is called discretionary money management, or what gives money managers the authority to buy and sell investments on their client's behalf based on their own decisions not their client's. Or you could specify a much broader range of powers, such as access to your bank accounts (what's known as a "general power of attorney").

Durable POA

A durable POA begins when it is signed but stays in effect for a lifetime unless you initiate the cancellation. Words in the document should specify that your agent's power should stay in effect even if you become incapacitated. Durable POAs are popular because the agent can manage affairs easily and inexpensively.

Springing POA

This POA comes into play only when a specific event occurs—your incapacitation, for instance. A springing power of attorney must be very carefully crafted to avoid any problems in identifying precisely when the triggering event has happened.

Medical POA

A medical POA, or durable power of attorney for healthcare decisions, or health care proxy, is both a durable and a springing POA. The springing aspect means that the POA takes effect only if specific conditions take place. As long as the principal is conscious, and of sound mind and body, the medical POA will not be triggered. Some medical POAs are written to end when the principal recovers from the incapacitating condition. You can have different POAs for different situations and appoint different agents to hold them as well.

A Will Is Not A POA

Do not expect your will to serve as a substitute for a power of attorney. A will designates the distribution of your property after death, while a POA is related to decisions made during your life.

However, you can have a living will in addition to a healthcare POA. A living will usually addresses specific issues and wishes related to medical treatment if you have a terminal condition, or related to dying (such as the extent to which lifesaving measures should be used).

A living will does not always deal with other important medical issues, however, such as whether you would decline dialysis or a blood transfusion. These are the kinds of concerns that can be directly articulated in a durable power of attorney for healthcare decisions.

Who Should Be Your Attorney-In-Fact?

The person you choose as your agent must be someone you trust without hesitation. Depending on how you've worded your POA, the person you select will have access to and be able to make decisions about your health, home, business affairs, personal property, and financial accounts.

It is useful to contact each institution you do business with to be certain that your POA authority will be honored. Some banks and financial institutions have their own forms to complete.

You may name more than one person to act as your agent and ask that they work together. However, bear in mind that they may not always have the same view of what needs to be done. You should also appoint a successor agent, in the event that the agent you originally chose cannot serve in that capacity when the need arises.

Signing a POA does not deprive you of control over your personal affairs. It is a contingency document that becomes a powerful instrument only when it is needed.

The Bottom Line

Choosing someone to hold your power of attorney and specifying that it will operate even if you lose capacity ensures that you have a plan in place for administering your financial and personal affairs if you are ever unable to do so.

This gives you more control over how that process will be handled should the need ever arise. If you move to another state, your power of attorney should remain effective; however, the American Bar Association recommends that you use such a move to update your power of attorney.

WHY SHOULD I HAVE A POWER OF ATTORNEY?

A power of attorney is a legal document that allows an individual to appoint another person or entity to act on their behalf to administer their affairs. The person who forms the power of attorney is known as the principal and the person granted the authority over the affairs is the attorney-in-fact. A power of attorney is in effect only as long as the principal is alive and it can only be enacted by a principal who is mentally competent.

You may think that once they have appointed a durable power of attorney you lose control of any decision making and how your assets are used. This is simply not true and the power of attorney only steps in if you are no longer mentally capable of running your personal, legal, and financial affairs.

A power of attorney form can be used to nominate a power of attorney to represent an individual and their affairs in several different areas should they become incapacitated.

The Three Main Roles of a Power of Attorney

- Making medical decisions on behalf of the principal
- Handling financial and legal matters on behalf of the principal
- Making decisions on the behalf of someone who has lost their mental capacity

Medical decisions for the principal can take place when the person has become unable to make those decisions for themselves due to incapacitation. This can also be called an advanced care directive and it grants authority to the attorney-in-fact to make medical decisions for the principal. It does not grant any other authority or powers to the attorney-in- fact other than administering to the healthcare needs of the principal.

An attorney-in-fact is not only appointed to handle the affairs of someone who has become incapacitated but can be appointed to act on the behalf of someone to handle a transaction. If a person does not have sufficient knowledge to manage a certain financial or legal matter, they can appoint an agent to handle that particular transaction on their behalf.

A power of attorney template can be created for any number of reasons that can include signing contracts, paying bills, buying and selling of stocks and bonds, managing real estate, and just about any type of matter that a person wishes to delegate to an agent.

A power of attorney template or POA form can be used to nominate a power of attorney to represent an individual and their affairs in several different areas should they become incapacitated.

It is unfortunate that as some of us age our mental abilities may be slowly lost before our physical abilities. In other cases, physical deterioration can occur before mental incapacity. You won't need a power of attorney if you are confined to a wheelchair or even bed-ridden provided your mental capacity is intact. A power of attorney needs to be prepared before you succumb to senility or dementia. The power of attorney completed in time ensures that your personal affairs are attended to when you no longer have the ability to manage them on your own. This includes legal and financial matters. This can prevent financial and family problems from occurring, especially if there has been inadequate estate planning by you, the principal.

WHAT POWERS DO MY ATTORNEYS HAVE?

A power of attorney for property can do anything on the grantor's behalf in respect of property that the grantor if capable could do, except make a will (for example pay bills, apply for benefits, or sell a home). A power of attorney for personal care can make decisions related to health care, nutrition, shelter, clothing, hygiene and safety. A person cannot act as attorney for personal care if they (1) provide health care to grantor for compensation; or (2) provides residential, social, training or support services to the grantor for compensation unless they are the grantor's spouse/partner/relative.

Who Can I Make My Power of Attorney?

People often appoint their spouse, relative, or a close friend with good judgment to be their attorney.

How Should I Choose My Attorney?

Below are some factors to consider when choosing a power of attorney for personal care and property.

Choose Someone Comfortable with The Responsibility

Being an attorney can be a stressful role, especially the attorney for personal care as they may have to make difficult decisions based on your state of health and well-being. This could include agreeing to, or refusing, certain medical procedures and life-saving interventions. They could also choose your accommodation, who interacts with you, who gives you care, and they may have full access to all of your medical records. They may even be called upon to represent you in court as your litigation guardian, should the matter at hand relate to your health or personal care.

Your attorney for property will need to make important decisions surrounding your finances and legal obligations. You'll want to choose someone organized and able to make critical decisions during a potentially stressful time. They will have the power to take possession of your property, using it to benefit you or your close family as they believe you would do if capable. They may also sell, rent, renovate, or otherwise manage your property, if it is what you would have done.

Choose Someone You Trust

Similar to choosing your executor, you'll want to select someone trustworthy, such as your spouse, a family member, relative or close friend. Remember that your attorney and executor do not have to be the same person, and they never act at the same time (one is making acting on your behalf while you're still alive, the other is acting on your behalf once you've passed away). These should be people with your best interests at heart, as they will have very broad powers to make decisions that affect your finances, healthcare, and day-to-day life.

Choose Someone Who Is Legally Able to Be Your Attorney

The person you choose should be a responsible adult, ideally someone accessible and living in a nearby city or town to you. While being a resident of Canada is not legally required, it's strongly recommended that the individual can be contacted quickly and can act with speed in an emergency. Typically, they must be over the age of majority in your province (18 in Ontario and Alberta, 19 in British Columbia)

Review Your Power of Attorney Regularly

Like your will, you should review and update your power of attorney documents as life changes. Monumental moments such as the birth or adoption of a child, moving to a new home, or divorce may trigger you to make changes to your documents.

Make sure your attorney is aware of the types of decisions they may need to make, so they will feel educated and confident to take on the responsibilities if called on.

Can I Choose More Than One Attorney?

With Willful you can only pick one attorney for property and one attorney for personal care. At the recommendation of our legal advisors, we do not currently allow multiple persons to be jointly nominated on the same tier, as it can lead to indecision and arguments in times of immediate need.

You can either have the same person appointed for both, or two different individuals. On Willful, you can have multiple layers of backups for each role should your first choice be unable or unwilling to act, or later decide that they cannot continue.

What Is a Power of Attorney Form?

A Power of Attorney form helps you formalize your wishes and choices of attorney or representative. Willful's dynamic platform can help create your personalized power of attorney documents so you know that your wishes will be carried out in the event that you are temporarily incapacitated. We will ask you questions such as your province of residence to ensure we are generating the right documentation and information for your current life situation. In addition, all Willful documents come with instructions on how to witness and sign your power of attorney documents to ensure they are legally-binding.

While certain will kits and government websites offer power of attorney forms, they are generally fill-in-the-blank documents and very cookie cutter. While these are cost-effective options, they may not account for your unique life situation. You will also need to take great care that the documents and method of witnessing is in compliance with the law in your province or territory.

Why Do I Need Two Different Power of Attorney Documents (Personal Care and Property)?

There are two types of powers of attorney: a power of attorney for personal care and a power of attorney for property.

Power Of Attorney for Property

The person described in this document will make decisions about your property and finances, such as paying your bills, managing your investments and collecting any money owed to you, if you are medically unable to do so yourself.

Power Of Attorney for Personal Care:

A spouse, relative or close friend with good judgment, the person described in this document will be the voice of your healthcare decisions if you are unable to communicate. This individual can make decisions regarding your health care, housing, meals, and clothing. This person will also communicate which life support measure you have outlined in your will.

What Makes a Power of Attorney Enduring or Continuing?

A general power of attorney ends immediately if you become mentally incapable or die. By contrast, enduring, or continuing, powers of attorney continue to have effect after the point of your mental incapacity. Attorneys nominated in these documents maintain their power to act if and when you become infirm, unable to communicate, or otherwise mentally incapable.

You are able to decide how much power you would like to give to your appointed attorney. Many Canadians use a limited power of attorney when they need assistance looking after their affairs due to traveling or if they are injured.

An enduring power of attorney, what we're referring to in this article, is a document you can use to appoint a person to make financial and legal decisions on your behalf. This type of POA continues if you were to become mentally incapable.

What is a Medical Directive and why everyone needs one?

CONTENTS

WHAT IS AN ADVANCE HEALTH CARE DIRECTIVE (AHCD)?

An advance directive is a general term for any document that provides directions about your health care when you can no longer speak for yourself.

Unfortunately, an advance directive is often thought of as a document that is designed exclusively for older people. That's not the case. Most "right-to-die" cases have involved young people. There is a misconception that healthy people don't need to have an advance directive, but it is important to develop a plan while you still have the capacity to do so.

Charles P. Sabatino is assistant director of the American Bar Association's Commission on Law and Aging and a past president of the National Academy of Elder Law Attorneys.

Advance directives can take many forms and the laws governing them are different in each state. A living will, for instance, lists your instructions about life-sustaining medical treatments you want to receive if you become terminally ill. A durable power of attorney for health care enables you to appoint someone as your health proxy to make health care decisions for you when you are incapacitated. Appointing a health care agent or proxy and talking to that person about your health care wishes, should be a priority Several advance directive forms are available. Select one with which you feel comfortable.

One form called "Five Wishes" covers these topics in non-legal terms and is becoming very popular.

More than just a legal document, an advance directive is an ongoing conversation about what's important to you. You can change it as your circumstances change. When you're young, you may not know what medical treatments you want, but you may be certain about who you want to make those decisions. If you're in your 70s or you have a serious illness and you know the course it is going to take, you may put in more detail.

While you don't necessarily need a lawyer to make an advance directive, an attorney is often in the best position to ensure that your stated wishes are followed. You may want to consult with an elder law attorney Elder law attorneys are specialists in health care and end-of-life decision-making. If you want to do it yourself, forms are available that comply with your state's requirements.

An advance health care directive or AHCD (otherwise known as a living will, personal directive, or medical directive) is a document that instructs others about your medical care should you be unable to make decisions on your own. It only becomes effective under the circumstances delineated in the document, and allows you to do either or both of the following:

Appoint A Health Care Agent

The advance directive allows you to appoint a health care agent (also known as "Durable Power of Attorney for Health Care," "Health Care Proxy," or "attorney-in-fact"), who will have the legal authority to make health care decisions for you if you are no longer able to speak for yourself. This is typically a spouse, but can be another family member, close friend, or anyone else you feel will ensure that your wishes and expectations are met. The individual named will have authority to make decisions regarding artificial nutrition and hydration and any other measures that prolong life—or not.

Prepare Instructions for Health Care.

The advance directive allows you to make specific written instructions for your future health care in the event of any situation in which you can no longer speak for yourself. It outlines your wishes about life-sustaining medical treatment if you are terminally ill or permanently unconscious, for example.

Although death is an inevitable part of life, many of us are reluctant to face the fact that we're not going to live forever and plan for our end-of-life care. The advance health care directive provides a clear statement of your wishes about prolonging your life or withholding or withdrawing treatment. You can also choose to request relief from pain even if doing so hastens death. A standard advance directive form provides room to state additional wishes and directions and allows you to leave instructions about organ donations and disposition of remains (burial or cremation). Discussing your wishes with loved ones and preparing an AHCD offers the best assurance that decisions regarding your future medical care will reflect your own values and desires.

WHY IS AN ADVANCE DIRECTIVE IMPORTANT?

While most people would prefer to die in their own homes, the norm is still for terminally ill patients to die in the hospital, often receiving ineffective treatments that they may not really want. Friends and family members often become embroiled in bitter arguments about the best way to care for the patient and consequently miss sharing the final stage of life with their loved one. And the opinions and wishes of the dying person are lost in all the chaos.

It's almost impossible to know what a dying person's wishes truly are unless they've been discussed ahead of time. Planning ahead with an advance directive can give your principal caregiver, family members, and other loved one's peace of mind when it comes to making decisions about your future health care. It lets everyone know what is important to you, and what is not. Talking about death with those close to you is not about being ghoulish or giving up on life, but a way to ensure greater quality of life, even when faced with a life-limiting illness or tragic accident. When your loved ones are clear about your preferences for treatment, they're free to devote their energy to care and compassion.

LIVING WILLS AND ADVANCE DIRECTIVES FOR MEDICAL DECISIONS

Plan ahead and get the medical care you want at the end of life.

Living wills and other advance directives are written, legal instructions regarding your preferences for medical care if you are unable to make decisions for yourself. Advance directives guide choices for doctors and caregivers if you're terminally ill, seriously injured, in a coma, in the late stages of dementia or near the end of life.

Advance directives aren't just for older adults. Unexpected end-of-life situations can happen at any age, so it's important for all adults to prepare these documents.

By planning ahead, you can get the medical care you want, avoid unnecessary suffering and relieve caregivers of decision-making burdens during moments of crisis or grief. You also help reduce confusion or disagreement about the choices you would want people to make on your behalf.

Power Of Attorney

A medical or health care power of attorney is a type of advance directive in which you name a person to make decisions for you when you are unable to do so. In some states this directive may also be called a durable power of attorney for health care or a health care proxy.

Depending on where you live, the person you choose to make decisions on your behalf may be called one of the following:

- Health care agent
- Health care proxy
- Health care surrogate
- Health care representative
- Health care attorney-in-fact
- Patient advocate

Choosing a person to act as your health care agent is important. Even if you have other legal documents regarding your care, not all situations can be anticipated, and some situations will require someone to make a judgment about your likely care wishes. You should choose a person who meets the following criteria:

- Meets your state's requirements for a health care agent
- Is not your doctor or a part of your medical care team?
- Is willing and able to discuss medical care and end-of-life issues with you
- Can be trusted to make decisions that adhere to your wishes and values
- Can be trusted to be your advocate if there are disagreements about your care

The person you name may be a spouse, other family member, friend or member of a faith community. You may also choose one or more alternates in case the person you chose is unable to fulfill the role.

Living Will

A living will is a written, legal document that spells out medical treatments you would and would not want to be used to keep you alive, as well as your preferences for other medical decisions, such as pain management or organ donation.

In determining your wishes, think about your values. Consider how important it is to you to be independent and self-sufficient and identify what circumstances might make you feel like your life is not worth living. Would you want treatment to extend your life in any situation? All situations? Would you want treatment only if a cure is possible?

You should address a number of possible end-of-life care decisions in your living will. Talk to your doctor if you have questions about any of the following medical decisions:

- **Cardiopulmonary resuscitation (CPR)** restarts the heart when it has stopped beating. Determine if and when you would want to be resuscitated by CPR or by a device that delivers an electric shock to stimulate the heart.

- **Mechanical ventilation** takes over your breathing if you're unable to breathe on your own. Consider if, when and for how long you would want to be placed on a mechanical ventilator.
- **Tube feeding** supplies the body with nutrients and fluids intravenously or via a tube in the stomach. Decide if, when and for how long you would want to be fed in this manner.
- **Dialysis** removes waste from your blood and manages fluid levels if your kidneys no longer function. Determine if, when and for how long you would want to receive this treatment.
- **Antibiotics or antiviral medications** can be used to treat many infections. If you were near the end of life, would you want infections to be treated aggressively or would you rather let infections run their course?
- **Comfort care (palliative care)** includes any number of interventions that may be used to keep you comfortable and manage pain while abiding by your other treatment wishes. This may include being allowed to die at home, getting pain medications, being fed ice chips to soothe mouth dryness, and avoiding invasive tests or treatments.
- **Organ and tissue donations** for transplantation can be specified in your living will. If your organs are removed for donation, you will be kept on life-sustaining treatment temporarily until the procedure is complete. To help your health care agent avoid any confusion, you may want to state in your living will that you understand the need for this temporary intervention.
- **Donating your body** for scientific study also can be specified. Contact a local medical school, university or donation program for information on how to register for a planned donation for research.

Do Not Resuscitate and Do Not Intubate Orders

You don't need to have an advance directive or living will to have do not resuscitate (DNR) and do not intubate (DNI) orders. To establish DNR or DNI orders, tell your doctor about your preferences. He or she will write the orders and put them in your medical record.

Even if you already have a living will that include your preferences regarding resuscitation and intubation, it is still a good idea to establish DNR or DNI orders each time you are admitted to a new hospital or health care facility.

Creating Advance Directives

Advance directives need to be in writing. Each state has different forms and requirements for creating legal documents. Depending on where you live, a form may need to be signed by a witness or notarized. You can ask a lawyer to help you with the process, but it is generally not necessary.

Links to state-specific forms can be found on the websites of various organizations such as the American Bar Association, AARP and the National Hospice and Palliative Care Organization.

Review your advance directives with your doctor and your health care agent to be sure you have filled out forms correctly. When you have completed your documents, you need to do the following:

- Keep the originals in a safe but easily accessible place.
- Give a copy to your doctor.
- Give a copy to your health care agent and any alternate agents.
- Keep a record of who has your advance directives.
- Talk to family members and other important people in your life about your advance directives and your health care wishes. By having these conversations now, you help ensure that your family members clearly understand your wishes. Having a clear understanding of your preferences can help your family members avoid conflict and feelings of guilt.
- Carry a wallet-sized card that indicates you have advance directives, identifies your health care agent and states where a copy of your directives can be found.
- Keep a copy with you when you are traveling.

Reviewing And Changing Advance Directives

You can change your directives at any time. If you want to make changes, you must create a new form, distribute new copies and destroy all old copies. Specific requirements for changing directives may vary by state.

You should discuss changes with your primary care doctor and make sure a new directive replaces an old directive in your medical file. New directives must also be added to medical charts in a hospital or nursing home. Also, talk to your health care agent, family and friends about changes you have made.

Consider reviewing your directives and creating new ones in the following situations:

- **New diagnosis.** A diagnosis of a disease that is terminal or that significantly alters your life may lead you to make changes in your living will. Discuss with your doctor the kind of treatment and care decisions that might be made during the expected course of the disease.
- **Change of marital status.** When you marry, divorce, become separated or are widowed, you may need to select a new health care agent.
- **About every 10 years.** Over time your thoughts about end-of-life care may change. Review your directives from time to time to be sure they reflect your current values and wishes.

Physician Orders for Life-Sustaining Treatment (POLST)

In some states, advance health care planning includes a document called physician orders for life-sustaining treatment (POLST). The document may also be called provider orders for life-sustaining treatment (POLST) or medical orders for life-sustaining treatment (MOLST).

A POLST is intended for people who have already been diagnosed with a serious illness. This form does not replace your other directives. Instead, it serves as doctor-ordered instructions — not unlike a prescription — to ensure that, in case of an emergency, you receive the treatment you prefer. Your doctor will fill out the form based on the contents of your advance directives, the discussions you have with your doctor about the likely course of your illness and your treatment preferences.

A POLST stays with you. If you are in a hospital or nursing home, the document is posted near your bed. If you are living at home or in a hospice care facility, the document is prominently displayed where emergency personnel or other medical team members can easily find it.

Forms vary by state, but essentially a POLST enables your doctor to include details about what treatments not to use, under what conditions certain treatments can be used, how long treatments may be used and when treatments should be withdrawn. Issues covered in a POLST may include:

- Resuscitation
- Mechanical ventilation
- Tube feeding
- Use of antibiotics
- Requests not to transfer to an emergency room
- Requests not to be admitted to the hospital
- Pain management

A POLST also indicates what advance directives you have created and who serves as your health care agent. Like advance directives, POLSTs can be canceled or updated.

DURABLE POWER OF ATTORNEY FOR HEALTH CARE

A durable power of attorney for health care is a signed, dated, and witnessed legal document commonly called a "health care proxy" or "health care power of attorney." This document differs from other durable powers of attorney in that it is specifically limited to health care and medically related decisions.

This document keeps your loved one in charge of his or her destiny. He or she appoints an individual—known as an "agent," or "proxy"—to make medical decisions in his or her behalf, if, and only if, your loved one becomes incapacitated and cannot make decisions for him or herself. The agent can be any competent adult—a family member, friend, or another person. Should your loved one ever become incapacitated due to illness or injury, the appointed agent will take over medical affairs and act within the guidelines and restrictions that your loved one has established.

A Durable Power of Attorney for Health Care Should:

- Adhere to the rules of the state in which it is created
- Include a backup if the original agent is not available
- Spell out clearly what matters the agent can and cannot handle

Principal And Agent

For caregivers, the "principal" will be your loved one, and you will be his or her "agent." Prior to signing a durable power of attorney for health care, the principal and agent must designate under what conditions the document becomes effective. As the agent, you would then be responsible for all medical matters until the principal's recovery or death. When your loved one signs a durable power of attorney for health care, make sure he or she communicates all wishes, values, and preferences to his or her agent. A lawyer can help your loved one understand how to tailor the durable power of attorney for health care to fit his or her wishes.

Combined Directives

Because the Living Will applies only in narrowly and sometimes unclearly defined circumstances, it may be in your loved one's best interest to have both a living will and a durable power of attorney for health care, or to combine them into one advance directive. In this case, the durable power of attorney states who should make the decisions, while the Living Will tells that agent what to decide.

Legal Requirements

Because different states have specific guidelines as to what an individual may or may not include in a living will and how to set up a health care power of attorney, it is advisable to consult with a lawyer or health care provider to obtain advice about the requirements that govern such documents in your loved one's state. Other good sources of legal information include your loved one's state's Attorney General's Office or Office on Aging. But while specific state laws may vary quite a bit, there are some general legal guidelines that apply in most cases.

Federal Law

In the United States, rights to advance medical directives are protected by the Federal Patient Self-Determination Act. This federal law requires hospitals, skilled nursing facilities, hospices, home health agencies, and managed care plans to give their patients who are covered by Medicare or Medicaid information about advance directives. The law is intended to increase a person's control over medical treatment decisions. However, health care providers only have to provide information about the laws for the state in which they are located. For more information, contact an Insurance Counseling Program for Medicare beneficiaries in your loved one's area.

Witnesses

In most states, advance directives must be signed in the presence of two people who then sign the document as witnesses. Each state has different requirements regarding who may or may not be a witness. In general, however, anyone who could stand to benefit from the person's death—such as beneficiaries of life insurance policies and/or heirs to the person's estate—

cannot be a witness. Many states also prohibit health care practitioners, including the person's doctor, attending nurses, and other professionals involved in health care, from being witnesses.

In order to avoid later challenges to an advance directive, your loved one should attempt to find witnesses who are not relatives, have no financial connections to him or her, and have no relationship to possible medical treatment. Your loved one should also make sure that any potential witnesses are familiar with his or her wishes, and that the witnesses will be available to appear at a hearing should the validity of the directive be challenged. Furthermore, witnesses need to be familiar enough with your loved one's condition that they can testify that your loved one was fully competent when he or she signed the document.

Competency

Most state statutes require that a person be "competent" or of "sound mind" in order to execute an advance directive. For states that offer a model form, a statement of competency is generally included. In addition, the model forms generally provide that witnesses who can affirm the competency of the individual must sign the document.

Some states also allow persons to draft a living will or other directive on behalf of incompetent adults. Such statutes often provide a list of individuals who are authorized to execute the document on behalf of the incompetent individual.

Forms

Some states with advance directive statutes provide a model document that may be followed. The model documents are standardized forms with blanks provided for the proper signatures. Any required witnesses should be present when an individual signs the document so that they can later confirm that the signature is an original. Witnesses may also be called upon to comment about the circumstances surrounding the signing, especially if there is concern that the individual was coerced into signing the document.

Some states require persons who wish to execute an advance directive to use their model form; others allow for modifications; and still others offer the model form only as a suggested guide. If your loved one lives in a state that provides a model form, it is a good idea for him or her to adhere to the model as closely as possible in order to prevent later objections to the implementation of the directive.

If your loved one wishes to specify additional directions to those provided on the model form, such directions should be written as an addendum to the model. This will ensure that the provisions of the basic document are enforced even if the additional directions are found to be invalid. To avoid the possibility of additional directions being found invalid, it is also wise to make sure that these provisions are written, signed, and witnessed in accordance with state requirements.

Duration

In some states, an advance medical directive doesn't take effect until it has been delivered to certain individuals. Generally, a copy must be provided to the physician responsible for treatment. A few states also require that the document filed with a state agency or with a state court. Your loved one should provide copies of any documents to all persons likely to be involved with his or her care. In addition, he or she should be sure to distribute copies to friends, family, and others who might be in a position to bring the document to the attention of the attending physician.

A properly executed advance directive will remain in force throughout your loved one's lifetime, unless revoked. Some states, however, impose a time limitation on how long a directive is effective without being re-executed. Most states also provide specific methods for revoking these documents. The methods vary and include any expression of your loved one's desire to revoke the document.

CREATING AN ADVANCE HEALTH CARE DIRECTIVE

Advance health care directives and living wills are not complicated, but the content can be complex and should be thought through very carefully. It can be short, simple statements about what you want done or not done if you can't speak for yourself.

It's important to discuss your wishes with family members as well as legal, health, or other appropriate professionals when preparing such a document. It is particularly important to talk about your wishes with everyone who might be involved in your care. In times of stress, others may confuse their own wishes with yours.

In the U.S., most state governments have designed forms for people to complete on their own by filling in the blanks. While these are not usually mandatory, most states do require witnessing or other specific signing formalities. Anything you write by yourself or with a computer software package should follow your state laws. So, it's essential for you to know what the specific laws are in your state or country.

Talking To Your Loved Ones About End-Of-Life Choices

To ensure that your future care wishes are understood and respected by all those who are important to you, it's imperative that you sit down and talk to your family and loved ones about your end-of-life choices.

For many of us, the prospect of such a conversation can seem like a daunting task. You or your loved ones may be uncomfortable talking about serious illness or death, or it may seem "too soon" to have a conversation about end-of-life preparations. However, it's better to have the conversation when you and your loved ones are in a calm and relaxed state, rather than in the midst of a medical emergency when everyone's stressed and it's difficult to think clearly.

While you may think that your loved ones already know what you want, the truth is there is often a startling difference between what people say they want and what their family members *think* they want. The only way to be certain that your loved ones understand your wishes is to sit down and have the conversation.

- **Choose a time and place where you and your loved ones feel comfortable** and at ease, such as after a family dinner, on a walk, or sitting outside in the sun.
- **Not everything has to be discussed at once**. The conversation can be spread out over different times.
- **Be patient with your loved ones**. Fear and denial are common. Some people need longer to become comfortable talking about dying, others may have different feelings about what end-of-life plans should involve.
- **Don't feel like you can never change your mind**. Your opinions and wishes can change over time and Advance Health Care Directives can be revised.

WHAT TO DO ONCE YOUR ADVANCE HEALTH CARE DIRECTIVE IS COMPLETE

Once you have completed your advance directive, it may be necessary to have it notarized depending on who witnesses your signature—follow the instructions on the document in accordance with your state laws. Providing many trusted individuals with copies of your advance directive will insure that your health care wishes are met in the event that you cannot express your wishes for yourself.

Keep the original copy of the advance directive yourself in a place that can easily be found, and give copies to:

- Your chosen health care proxy (with directions on where to find the original).
- Family members or other loved ones.
- Your primary care physician, hospital, or health care institution. Ask that a copy is placed in your medical record and make sure your doctor will support your wishes.
- Anyone named in the directive.

A copy can also be sent to your attorney or kept in a safety deposit box or anywhere else you keep copies of a will or other important papers. Be sure that you have discussed the directive with the person you designate as your health care agent and that they understand your wishes and the responsibilities involved and will agree to honor those wishes.

What Happens If I Change My Mind?

It's best to think of Advance Health Care Directives as a work in progress. Circumstances can change, as can your values and opinions about how you would best like your future health care needs to be met. Directives can be revoked or replaced at any time as long as you are capable of making your own decisions.

It is recommended that you review your documents every few years or after important life changes and revise your directives to ensure that they continue to accurately reflect your situation and wishes.

When To Reassess Your Advance Directive

Re-examine your health care wishes every few years or whenever any of the "Five D's" occur:

1. **Decade** – when you start each new decade of your life.
2. **Death** – whenever you experience the death of a loved one.
3. **Divorce** – when you experience a divorce or other major family change.
4. **Diagnosis** – when you are diagnosed with a serious health condition.
5. **Decline** – when you experience a significant decline or deterioration of an existing health condition, especially when it diminishes your ability to live independently.

Choices about end of life are important for all adults—not just for the older population. Not only does an advance health care directive let your voice be heard about what you want, but it also relieves others of making these decisions for you.

Changing Your Advance Directive

If your current advance health care directive no longer reflects your wishes for end-of-life care, refer to your state's (or country's) laws for the correct way to cancel or amend the directive. Once you have revised the directive, it is important to discuss the changes with your physician and family members and notify everyone who has copies of your old directive.

WHAT IS A WILL AND WHY DO I NEED ONE NOW?

Contents

WHAT IS A WILL?

A Will, also known as a Last Will and Testament, is a legally prepared and bound document that states your intentions for the distribution of your assets and wealth after your death. In the event you have children, a valid Will also allows you to designate who will care for them. A Will, however, is only one part of a comprehensive Estate Plan.

The history of Wills actually dates back to Ancient Roman times. The idea was based around the desire to provide instructions for the passing of one's possessions to Beneficiaries. Interestingly, many of the original 19th century requirements that were established in England surrounding the creation of Last Will and Testaments have withstood the test of time and are still legal requirements to this day in many states.

In the simplest terms, a properly prepared Will is a legal document that ensures you're protecting your assets, surviving spouse and heirs after you pass. By explicitly outlining what you want to have happen in the future, your final wishes will not be ignored if others try to step in.

The Document Spells Out Who Should Get Your Assets After Your Death

A Will is a legal document that sets forth your wishes regarding the distribution of your property and the care of any minor children. If you die without a Will, those wishes may not be carried out. Further, your heirs may end up spending additional time, money, and emotional energy to settle your affairs after you're gone.

Wills can vary in their effectiveness, depending on the type, though no document will likely resolve every issue that arises after your death. Here's what you need to know about these vital documents.

WHY YOU SHOULD HAVE A WILL

Some people think that only the very wealthy or those with complicated assets need Wills. However, there are many good reasons to have a Will.

- You can be clear about who gets your assets. You can decide who gets what and how much.
- You can keep your assets out of the hands of people you don't want to have them (like an estranged relative).
- You can identify who should care for your children. Without a Will, the courts will decide.
- Your heirs will have a faster and easier time getting access to your assets.
- You can plan to save your estate money on taxes. You can also give gifts and charitable donations, which can help offset the estate tax.

A Written, Witnessed Will Is Best

To maximize the likelihood that your wishes will be carried out, create what's known as a Testamentary Will. This is the most familiar type of Will; you prepare the document and then sign it in witnesses' presence. It's arguably the best insurance against successful challenges to your wishes by family members or business associates after you die. You can write one yourself, but have it prepared by a trusts and estates attorney for greater insurance.

OTHER TYPES OF INHERITANCE WILLS

While a Testamentary Willis likely your best bet, several other types of Wills get varying degrees of recognition.

Holographic Wills

Wills written and signed by the testator but not witnessed are known as Holographic Wills—from the less common secondary meaning of the word holograph, meaning a document hand-written by its author. Such Wills are often used when time is short and witnesses are unavailable, for example, when the testator is trapped in a life-threatening accident.

Holographic Wills are not recognized in some states, however. In states that permit the documents, the Will must meet minimal requirements, such as proof that the testator wrote it and had the mental capacity to do so. Even then, the absence of witnesses often leads to challenges to the Will's validity.

Oral Wills

Least widely recognized are oral Wills, in which the testator speaks their wishes before witnesses. Lacking a written record, or at least one prepared by the testator, courts do not widely recognize oral Wills.

Pour-Over Wills

Another type of Will, a pour-over Will, is used in conjunction with creating a trust into which your assets flow.

Mutual Wills

A married or committed couple usually executes this type of Will. After one party dies, the remaining party is bound by the terms of the mutual Will.

Mutual Wills can be used to ensure that property passes to the deceased's children rather than to a new spouse. Because of state differences in contract law, a mutual will should be established with a legal professional's help. Though the terms sound similar, a mutual Will should not be confused with a joint Will.

WHAT DOES A WILL COVER?

A Will allows you to direct how your belongings—such as bank balances, property, or prized possessions—should be distributed. If you have a business or investments, your will can specify who will receive those assets and when.

A Will also allows you to direct assets to a charity (or charities) of your choice. Similarly, if you wish to leave assets to an institution or an organization, a Will can assure that your wishes are carried out.

While Wills generally address the bulk of your assets, some aren't covered by their instructions. Those omissions include payouts from the testator's life insurance policy. Since the policy has specified beneficiaries, those individuals will receive the proceeds. The same Will likely apply for any investment accounts that are designated as "transfer on death."

There's a key exception: If the beneficiaries of those assets predeceased the testator, the policy or account then reverts to the estate and is distributed according to the terms of a Will or, failing that, by a probate court—a part of the judicial system that primarily handles Wills, estates, and related matters.

Most states have elective-share or community property laws that prevent people from disinheriting their spouses. If a Will assigns a smaller proportion of such assets to the surviving spouse than state law specifies, which is typically between 30% and 50%, a court may override the Will.

In addition to directing your assets, a Will states your preferences for who should take over as guardian for your minor children in the event of your death.

What Happens if I Don't Have a Will?

If you die intestate—that is, without a Will —the state oversees the dispensation of your assets, which it will typically distribute according to a set formula.

Because of the elective-share and community property provisions mentioned above, the formula often results in half of your estate going to your spouse and the other half going to your children. Such a scenario sometimes results in the sale of the family home or other assets, which can negatively affect a surviving spouse who may have counted on the bulk of your assets to maintain their standard of living.

Further complications may ensue if your children are minors, as the court will appoint a representative to look after their interests.

Dying intestate may have tax consequences, too, since a properly prepared Will can reduce the estate tax liability. As of 2021, a U.S. estate tax return must be filed on individual estates valued at $11,700,000 or more. No federal estate tax is due if the estate is worth less than that amount.

GETTING STARTED ON YOUR WILL

To prepare a Will, begin by compiling a list of your assets and debts. Be sure to include the contents of safe deposit boxes, family heirlooms, and other assets that you wish to transfer to a particular person or entity.

If you wish to leave particular personal property to specific heirs, begin a list of those allocations for eventual inclusion in your Will. Besides, you can identify the recipients of specific assets in a separate document called a letter of instruction, kept with the Will. However, if you include assignments only within this letter, check that the document is legally binding where you live; some states do not recognize them.

The letter of instruction can be written more informally than the Will. It can also include specifics that will help your executor settle your estate, including account numbers, passwords, and even burial instructions. Other addenda to the Will, such as power of attorney, a medical directive, or a Living Will , can direct the court on handling matters if a person becomes physically or mentally incapacitated.

If both you and your spouse lack Wills, you might be tempted to prepare a single document that covers you both. Resist the temptation. Estate planners almost universally advise against joint Wills, and some states don't even recognize them. Separate wills make more sense, even if your Will and that of your spouse may end up looking remarkably similar. (As noted above, a joint Will is not to be confused with a mutual Will.)

How To Prepare and Validate Your Will

You don't necessarily need professional help to prepare a valid Will. If you are comfortable taking care of the task on your own, several software programs are available to assist you, as are various DIY websites. Once you've drafted the document, it needs to be witnessed, usually by two adults of sound mind who know you well.

Any person may act as a witness to your Will, but it's best to pick what's known as a disinterested witness—someone who isn't a beneficiary and has no financial or personal stake in your choices. Some states require two or more witnesses. If a lawyer prepared the Will, they shouldn't serve as one of the witnesses.

In some states, a Will must also be notarized, so check the rules where you live. Even if that formality isn't required, you might consider having your witnesses complete what's known as a self-proving affidavit. Signed in the presence of a notary, the document may facilitate the probate process by reducing the likelihood witnesses will be called into court to validate their signatures and the Will's authenticity.

CHOOSING AN EXECUTOR FOR YOUR WILL

You'll need to name a still-living person as the executor of the estate. That person, often a spouse, adult child, or another trusted friend or relative, is responsible for administering the estate. You can also name joint executors, such as your spouse or partner and your attorney.

The probate court usually supervises the executor to ensure that they carry out the wishes specified in the Will. If your affairs are complicated, it might make more sense to name an attorney or someone with legal and financial expertise.

The case for engaging an attorney is strong if your estate is substantial (ranging in the millions of dollars) or your situation is legally complex. If so, be sure to work with someone who is familiar with your state's laws and has extensive experience with writing wills. Your state bar association may be able to help you locate a suitable attorney.

One of the most important things your Will can do is empower your executor to pay your bills and deal with debt collectors. Ensure the wording of the Will allows for this and gives your executor leeway to take care of any related issues that aren't explicitly outlined in your Will.

Where To Keep a Will

A probate court usually requires access to your original Will before it can process your estate. It's crucial, then, to keep the document where it is safe and yet accessible. Avoid storing it in a bank safety deposit box or in any other location where your family may need a court order to gain access. A waterproof and fireproof safe in your house is a good alternative.

Then let at least your executor know where the original Will is stored, along with needed information such as the password for the safe. Besides, it's wise to duplicate signed copies to the executor and your attorney if you have one. The signed copies can be used to establish your intentions in case the original is destroyed or lost. However, the absence of an original Will can complicate matters, and without it, there's no guarantee that your estate will be settled as you'd hoped. So, store the document with care.

HOW TO CHANGE A WILL

Your will may never need to be updated. Or you may choose to update it regularly. Remember, the only version of your Will that matters is the most current valid one in existence at the time of your death.

A good rule of thumb: Review your will every two or three years and at pivotal moments in your life. Such events might include marriage, divorce, or the birth of a child. Your kids probably won't need guardians named in a will after they're adults, for example.

Changing your Will is easy. You write a new Will to replace the old one or make an addition using an amendment known as a codicil. Because of the serious nature of codicils and their power to change the entire Will, two witnesses are usually required to sign when a codicil is added, much like when the original Will was created. Some states, however, have loosened the legal regulations surrounding codicils and now allow for them to be notarized at a public notary.

Ideally, you want to make any changes when you are of sound mind and in good health. This limits the likelihood that your wishes can be successfully challenged and avoids decisions made in haste or under intense emotional pressure.

THE 10 MOST IMPORTANT REASONS TO HAVE A WILL

A Last Will and Testament is a legal document that lets you decide what happens with your estate after you die. Yet, according to a recent survey, almost two-thirds of all Americans don't have a Will.

If you're among them, you should know that there are many reasons to have a Will. When you die without a Will , you leave important decisions up to a local court and your state's laws. You won't have a say in who receives your property and other assets. Plus, not having a will can make it more difficult for your loved ones after you pass.

Here are the top ten reasons you should make a will today:

1. Save time, money, and stress for your loved ones.

Almost all estates have to go to probate court to start the legal process overseeing the distribution of assets. But when you don't have a Will, this process can get especially complicated. The court has to name a personal representative to administer your estate. And this can be time-consuming, expensive, and even contentious for your loved ones.

One of the top reasons to have a Will is to streamline this probate process. When you have a Will, you can choose the person you want to handle your estate, making it easier for your loved ones.

2. Determine who will manage your estate.

As mentioned above, deciding who will handle your estate is a great reason to have a Will. When you write a Will, you become a "testator" and have the opportunity to nominate an "executor." This is the person who will be in charge of wrapping up all your affairs.

Being an executor is an important job. Their responsibilities may include everything from closing bank accounts to liquidating assets. So, you should choose someone who is capable and who you trust to carry out these activities. If you don't choose an executor in your Will, the court will pick one for you — and it may not be the person you'd want.

3. **Decide who gets your assets and property — and who does not.**

Most people know that a Will lets them decide who will get their property. As the testator, you can name people as beneficiaries for specific assets. You can also name beneficiaries for any property that you don't list — the "residuary" of your estate. When your executor handles your will, they'll be in charge of distributing these assets.

You might not be aware that you can also use a Will to help ensure that some people don't receive anything. For example, you might want to prevent an ex-spouse from receiving an inheritance. Or, if one child received your support through school, you might want to make sure a second child gets their fair share, too.

4. Choose who will take care of your minor children.

If you're a parent, you can use your Will to nominate a guardian for your minor children. The surviving parent will usually get sole legal custody if one parent dies. But if both parents pass, this is one of the most important reasons to have a Will.

A guardian will be responsible for all your children's daily needs, including food, housing, health care, education, and clothing. And if you don't nominate a guardian in your Will, a court will have to choose one for you. This could mean that someone you would not have chosen will be raising your kids.

5. Provide a home for your pets.

Owning a pet is a great reason to have a Will. With a Will, you can make sure that someone takes care of your pet after you die. The law considers pets to be property, so you can't leave any assets to your pet with your Will. But you can name a beneficiary for your pet, leaving them to a trusted friend or family member. You can ask that person to act as a caretaker or guardian for your pet, and even leave them funds to provide for your pet's care.

6. Leave instructions for your digital assets.

Your digital assets may include online accounts, such as Facebook or email, and digital files or property (photos, videos, domain names, etc). In your Will, you can name a digital executor to manage these assets after you pass. You can leave them to specific people, and also include information on how you want them handled (e.g. if you'd like an account closed).

7. Lower the potential for family disputes.

If you have complicated family dynamics, there's a good reason to have a Will. When you die without a Will, your family will have to guess at what your final wishes were. And chances are, they won't always agree. This ambiguity can create friction, and even fights, which sometimes lasts a lifetime. Creating a Will solves the problem by eliminating the guesswork.

8. Support your favorite causes and leave a legacy.

Many people want to leave a positive impact on the world after they pass. And a great way to do this is to support the charities or causes you love most. When you write a Will, you can preserve your legacy by leaving a part of your estate to a charitable organization.

If you use FreeWill to make your Will, this is super simple to do. Our tool allows you to select your favorite causes with just a few clicks.

9. Provide funeral instructions.

You may not want to think about your own funeral. But if you do think about it now, and leave instructions with your Will , you can lessen the burden on your loved ones after you pass. While these instructions aren't legally binding, they can give your trustees some guidance on your wishes.

When you include instructions, you can name a funeral executor to manage the process, give suggestions for the service and location, make requests for your final resting place, and more.

10. It's easy to make a Will and gain peace of mind.

Some folks put off creating or updating their Will because they assume their loved ones will automatically get an inheritance. But this isn't always true. Probate can be a long and expensive process for your heirs. Plus, a Will only addresses your current circumstances. You should update it over time as your needs and the people in your life change.

When you create or update your Will, you can look after your loved ones and give them an easy map to follow after you pass. This gives many people peace of mind, making it one of the most important reasons to have a Will.

WHAT'S INCLUDED IN A WILL?

While there are many different types of Wills, there are some main components that all will likely include.

- **Executo**r: When you name an Executor, you are determining who will be in charge of making sure the wishes expressed in your Will are followed. Your Executor can be your spouse, another adult family member, a close friend, a lawyer or even an adult child. You can also specify Joint Executors.
- **Guardianship:** For parents, appointing a guardian is often one of the biggest motivations for establishing a Will. The peace of mind that comes from knowing you've selected the best person possible to look after your children is priceless.

- **Assets**: A Will establishes where and how your assets or personal property go to your heirs. It gives you the opportunity to specify who gets what from your estate.
- **Real Property**: Any building, structure or home that you own at the time of your passing is considered "real property." Sometimes, it makes sense to create a Trust that owns any real property.
- **Final Arrangements Instructions**: Specifying funeral arrangements and your wishes for your remains is a big part of your Estate Planning.

Who Can Be My Executor?

- You can name a beneficiary as your executor.
- An executor must be at least 18 years of age.
- You can name a friend or relative as your executor. If they need help they can seek the assistance of a lawyer or other professional.
- It is often a good idea to appoint joint executors.
- You can choose a lawyer to act as executor. Their cost will vary depending on how much work they must do.

A trustee company will charge a percentage of your estate (up to 6%) to be your executor. This charge does not vary according to the amount of work involved.

Where the executor may need to do ongoing work, for example, as a trustee for a child or a disabled adult, a trustee company may be preferable to a lawyer. Remember when naming an executor that problems might arise if they die before you and you haven't made another Will. You may choose a trustee company or someone who will be able to carry out your wishes and who you think will live longer than you.

What Happens When I Die?

It is the executor's job to carry out your wishes as stated in your Will, including any funeral arrangements you may have specified. After your death, your executor must carry out certain legal procedures. As a general rule, if you leave more than $10,000 or if you leave land in your name only it will be necessary for your executor to apply for probate.

Probate is the official court declaration that a will is to be treated as valid and binding. Your executor must pay your debts from your estate (such as funeral expenses, bills, etc.).

Beneficiaries will only receive something after all the bills are paid. If you die and there is not enough money to pay all your debts, your funeral and executor's expenses are paid before other debts. Your beneficiaries do not have to pay your debts, nor does your executor. When a beneficiary dies before you and you have left them a specific gift, the gift lapses. If you did not nominate a substitute beneficiary to get that gift, then it will go to the person(s) you have named to get the rest of your property, after the specific gifts have been made.

Contesting A Will

You can contest a Will if the person who made the Will was of unsound mind or if he or she could not freely choose what to put in their Will because another person unfairly influenced them. Another reason to contest a Will is if the meaning is unclear. Anyone with a possible interest in the estate can challenge a Will for these reasons.

- Often people wish to contest a Will because they consider it to be unfair.
- Who can apply to challenge an unfair Will?
- If you decide to contest the Will you will have to show the court that the deceased failed to provide for your proper maintenance. The court will look at how much money was in the estate and how much money you would receive. The court has very wide powers to look at all the circumstances including how well you got on with the deceased and also whether you helped look after them.

Remember if the court gives you more money, then others will get less.

The court will have to consider these people and their entitlements in comparison to your claim. Essentially, the court will have to consider whether the deceased had a moral duty to provide for you. The law is very complicated in this area. If you believe you may have a claim you should seek legal advice as soon as possible.

DIFFERENCES BETWEEN A WILL AND A TRUST

There is one major difference between a Will and a Trust. A Trust takes effect as soon as it's created and signed, but a Will does so after you pass away. There are some other differences as well, including:

- Wills require probate in order to transfer items to designated beneficiaries, whereas Trusts (both irrevocable and revocable) can avoid this.
- Wills are public record while Trusts remain private.
- Wills only take effect after your passing, but because a Trust is immediately effective, it can provide direction while you're alive in the event you become unable to make decisions on your own.

STEPS FOR CREATING A WILL

Regardless of which route you take to create your Will, there are some basic steps you want to take to ensure you're covering everything you need, so your final wishes will be known and adhered to.

1. Take inventory of your assets. Everything from your home to your personal items — and don't forget about digital assets!
2. Choose your Beneficiaries. Decide which items you want to distribute to which people.
3. Select an Executor. Choose your person and notify them of your choice.
4. Decide on who you will appoint as guardian if you have children. This step is only necessary if you have minor children or grandchildren.
5. Be explicit. It's important to be extremely specific about how your assets will be passed down so that your final wishes are carried out appropriately.

6. Make your Will online if you decide to forego the traditional attorney route. You have many options here, so it's important to find someone trustworthy. Look for a partner who understands the nuances and complexities of Estate Planning.
7. Sign and notarize your Will. Two witnesses are required in most states, but there are some, such as Vermont, that require more.
8. Put your Will in a safe place. A fireproof safe is the best option. Some people opt to use a safe deposit box at a bank, but there is a downside to this – it can be difficult to access safe deposit boxes after an owner dies.

Make updates to your Will. This should happen periodically as needed but recommended to do so every 3 to 5 years or after important life events.

What Should You Not Put in Your Will?

There are certain things you can't or shouldn't put in your Will. For example, a Will shouldn't have:

- Property that's jointly held
- Funeral plans (Though Final Arrangement plans can be put in a Will, there is some debate about this. If you choose to include your wishes for your funeral plans in your Will, it's advisable to also put them somewhere else, as sometimes plans left solely in a Will may be found too late.)
- Life insurance (You will have designated a Beneficiary on individual life insurance policies.)
- Retirement funds (Similar to life insurance, you should designate a Beneficiary who will receive your retirement funds upon your passing.)
- Digital estate items (The advent of technology has introduced a new concept in Estate Planning: the idea of a "digital estate," which includes things you've purchased digitally, like your cloud-based accounts, iTunes purchases, eBooks, videos, etc. While these can't effectively be put in a Will, you can note a "Digital Executor," who will have expressed authority to handle your digital accounts)

CREATING A LAST WILL: PROS AND CONS

Most people have feelings—often strong ones—about who should receive their assets after they're gone. But many put off making a Will until it's too late. The good news is that making a Will is much simpler and more affordable than most people think. But first, you should know the pros and cons.

No one wants to think about a time when they'll no longer be around, but planning for the inevitable—that is, setting down your wishes in as last Will —can not only give you peace of mind, it can also make things easier on your family and friends.

Having a last Will in place at the time of your death is a smart choice, but as with everything, there are advantages and disadvantages to consider when drafting one. Some of these pros and cons are discussed below.

Advantages Of a Last Will

You can leave property to those you choose.

One of the greatest advantages to having a Will is that you can choose who will receive what from your estate. Without a Will, your estate is subject state laws of "intestacy." That means the people you would like to benefit may receive little or nothing, while others with whom you're not as close receive the bulk. Accordingly, if you are not married but have a long-term partner, he or she could receive nothing under such laws. Alternately, if you are in the process of a divorce but it has not been finalized, without a Will, your estranged husband or wife could make a claim on your estate.

You can name a guardian for children and provide for them.

A Will allows you to choose a guardian for your children and set aside funds to make sure of their support and comfort.

You can create a testamentary trust in the Will.

You can create a testamentary trust within a last Will, which is created upon your death and used to hold property for another person's benefit, such as your children.

You choose your executor.

The executor is in charge of making sure all your bequests are carried out. A Will gives you complete control over deciding who this will be. The executor should be someone who is willing and able to handle everything that is involved with the closing of your estate. Without a Will, a court appoints someone to administer your estate, and that person may not be someone you would choose.

You can plan for personal matters.

From burial arrangements to pet care, you can use a Will to dictate what type of services, if any, you would like, and other personal matters.

You can amend it.

Circumstances change, and so can your Will. Through a "codicil," you can amend any provisions of your Will at any time so that they better reflect your most current wishes and assets.

You can revoke it.

If you find that a Will no longer represents your interests, you can revoke it entirely and start over.

Doesn't have to be expensive.

Creating a Will can be surprisingly affordable, particularly if your finances, assets and beneficiaries are fairly straightforward.

Disadvantages of a Last Will

Possible challenges.

Although it's possible that someone could challenge your Will, if you have followed all of the proper procedures in its creation, your Will and its provisions will likely stand.

May need to go through probate.

If you have assets that pass under your Will worth more than a certain amount, your Will must be filed for probate, the procedure through which a decedent's assets are distributed; this can be a long process, which can, in turn, be costly for the estate. In contrast, a living trust does not require probate.

It is public record.

A Will becomes public record once it is filed for probate, which means anyone can search for it and see its contents.

May not fully address tax concerns.

A Will that is not carefully planned out could leave your estate open to paying large state and/or federal estate taxes or your beneficiaries to paying hefty inheritance taxes. LegalZoom's Last Wills include provisions helping to minimize state and federal estate taxes.

Final Thoughts on Last Wills

All of the disadvantages listed above can be addressed with proper will planning and/or other estate planning documents, so don't let the potential downsides discourage you from expressing your last wishes in writing.

Also, laws regarding last Wills do vary by state, so it is crucial that you understand the requirements for drafting and signing a valid Will in your jurisdiction to avoid further problems in its execution.

California Last Will and Testament
of

____

Pursuant to Title 28 - Wills, Estates, and Fiduciary Relationships

I, ______________________, resident in the City of __________________, County of __________________, State of California being of sound mind, not acting under duress or undue influence, and fully understanding the nature and extent of all my property and of this disposition thereof, do hereby make, publish, and declare this document to be my Last Will and Testament, and hereby revoke any and all other wills and codicils heretofore made by me.

I. EXPENSES & TAXES

I direct that all my debts, and expenses of my last illness, funeral, and burial, be paid as soon after my death as may be reasonably convenient, and I hereby authorize my Personal Representative, hereinafter appointed, to settle and discharge, in his or her absolute discretion, any claims made against my estate.

I further direct that my Personal Representative shall pay out of my estate any and all estate and inheritance taxes payable by reason of my death in respect of all items included in the computation of such taxes, whether passing under this Will or otherwise. Said taxes shall be paid by my Personal Representative as if such taxes were my debts without recovery of any part of such tax payments from anyone who receives any item included in such computation.

II. PERSONAL REPRESENTATIVE

I nominate and appoint ________________________, of ____________________________, County of ________________________, State of ______________________________ as Personal Representative of my estate and I request that (he/she) be appointed temporary Personal Representative if (he/she) applies. If my Personal Representative fails or ceases to so serve, then I nominate ______________________________of ________________________, County of ____________________________, State of ______________________ to serve.

III. DISPOSITION OF PROPERTY

I devise and bequeath my property, both real and personal and wherever situated, as follows:

1st Beneficiary

______________________ [full name], currently of ______________________ [address], as my ______________________ [relation] whose last four (4) digits of their Social Security Number (SSN) are xxx-xx-_____ with the following property:

____

2nd Beneficiary

______________________ [full name], currently of ______________________ [address], as my ______________________ [relation] whose last four (4) digits of their Social Security Number (SSN) are xxx-xx-_____ with the following property:

____

3rd Beneficiary

_________________________ [full name], currently of _________________________ [address], as my _________________________ [relation] whose last four (4) digits of their Social Security Number (SSN) are xxx-xx-_____ with the following property:

____

If any of my beneficiaries have pre-deceased me, then any property that they would have received if they had not pre-deceased me shall be distributed in equal shares to the remaining beneficiaries.

If any of my property cannot be readily sold and distributed, then it may be donated to any charitable organization or organizations of my Personal Representative's choice. If any property cannot be readily sold or donated, my Personal Representative may, without liability, dispose of such property as my Personal Representative may deem appropriate. I authorize my Personal Representative to pay as an administration expense of my estate the expense of selling, advertising for sale, packing, shipping, insuring and delivering such property.

IV. OMISSION

Except to the extent that I have included them in this Will, I have intentionally, and not as a result of any mistake or inadvertence, omitted in this Will to provide for any family members and/or issue of mine, if any, however defined by law, presently living or hereafter born or adopted.

V. BOND

No bond shall be required of any fiduciary serving hereunder, whether or not specifically named in this Will, or if a bond is required by law, then no surety will be required on such bond.

VI. DISCRETIONARY POWERS OF PERSONAL REPRESENTATIVE

My Personal Representative, shall have and may exercise the following discretionary powers in addition to any common law or statutory powers without the necessity of court license or approval:

A. To retain for whatever period my Personal Representative deems advisable any property, including property owned by me at my death, and to invest and reinvest in any property, both real and personal, regardless of whether any particular investment would be proper for a Personal Representative and regardless of the extent of diversification of the assets held hereunder.

B. To sell and to grant options to purchase all or any part of my estate, both real and personal, at any time, at public or private sale, for consideration, whether or not the highest possible consideration, and upon terms, including credit, as my Personal Representative deems advisable, and to execute, acknowledge, and deliver deeds or other instruments in connection therewith.

C. To lease any real estate for terms and conditions as my Personal Representative deems advisable, including the granting of options to renew, options to extend the term or terms, and options to purchase.

D. To pay, compromise, settle or otherwise adjust any claims, including taxes, asserted in favor of or against me, my estate or my Personal Representative.

E. To make any separation into shares in whole or in part in kind and at values determined by my Personal Representative, with or without regard to tax basis, and to allocate different kinds and disproportionate amounts of property and undivided interests in property among the shares.

F. To make such elections under the tax laws as my Personal Representative shall deem appropriate, including elections with respect to qualified terminable interest property, exemptions and the use of deductions as income tax or estate tax deductions, and to determine whether to make any adjustments between income and principal on account of any election so made.

G. To make any elections permitted under any pension, profit sharing, employee stock ownership or other benefit plan.

H. To employ others in connection with the administration of my estate, including legal counsel, investment advisors, brokers, accountants and agents and to pay reasonable compensation in addition to my Personal Representative's compensation.

I. To vote any shares of stock or other securities in person or by proxy; to assert or waive any stockholder's rights or privilege to subscribe for or otherwise acquire additional stock; to deposit securities in any voting trust or with any committee.

J. To borrow and to pledge or mortgage any property as collateral, and to make secured or unsecured loans. My Personal Representative is specifically authorized to make loans without interest to any beneficiary hereunder. No individual or entity loaning property to my Personal Representative or trustee shall be held to see to the application of such property.

K. My Personal Representative shall also in his or her absolute discretion determine the allocation of any GST exemption available to me at my death to property passing under this Will or otherwise. The determination of my Personal Representative with respect to any elections or allocation, if made or taken in good faith, shall be binding upon all affected.

VII. CONTESTING BENEFICIARY

If any beneficiary under this Will, or any trust herein mentioned, contests or attacks this Will or any of its provisions, any share or interest in my estate given to that contesting beneficiary under this Will is revoked and shall be disposed of in the same manner provided herein as if that contesting beneficiary had predeceased me.

VIII. GUARDIAN AD LITEM NOT REQUIRED

I direct that the representation by a guardian ad litem of the interests of persons unborn, unascertained or legally incompetent to act in proceedings for the allowance of accounts hereunder be dispensed with to the extent permitted by law.

IX. GENDER

Whenever the context permits, the term "Personal Representative" shall include "Executor" and "Administrator," the use of a particular gender shall include any other gender, and references to the singular or the plural shall be interchangeable. All references to the Internal Revenue Code shall mean the Internal Revenue Code of 1986 or any successor Code. All references to estate taxes shall include inheritance and other death taxes.

X. ASSIGNMENT

The interest of any beneficiary in this Will, shall not be alienable, assignable, attachable, transferable nor paid by way of anticipation, nor in compliance with any order, assignment or covenant and shall not be applied to, or held liable for, any of their debts or obligations either in law or equity and shall not in any event pass to his, her, or their assignee under any instrument or under any insolvency or bankruptcy law, and shall not be subject to the interference or control of creditors, spouses or others.

XI. GOVERNING LAW

This document shall be governed by the laws in the State of California

XII. BINDING ARRANGEMENT

Any decision by my Personal Representative with respect to any discretionary power hereunder shall be final and binding on all persons interested. Unless due to my Executor's own willful default or gross negligence, no Executor shall be liable for said Executor's acts or omissions or those of any co-Executor or prior Executor.

I, the undersigned ________________________, do hereby declare that I sign and execute this instrument as my last Will, that I sign it willingly in the presence of each of the undersigned witnesses, and that I execute it as my free and voluntary act for the purposes herein expressed, on this ____ day of ________________, 20____.

______________________________	______________________________
Testator Signature	Testator (Printed Name)

The foregoing instrument, was on this ____ day of ________________, 20____, subscribed on each page and at the end thereof by ________________________, the above-named Testator, and by (him/her) signed, sealed, published and declared to be (his/her) LAST WILL AND TESTAMENT, in the presence of us and each of us, who thereupon, at (his/her) request, in (his/her) presence, and in the presence of each other, have hereunto subscribed our names as attesting witnesses thereto.

______________________________	______________________________
Witness Signature	Address
______________________________	______________________________
Witness Signature	Address

TESTAMENTARY AFFIDAVIT

STATE OF ____________________

COUNTY OF ___________________, SS.

Before me, the undersigned authority, on this day personally appeared ___________, testator, _____________________, witness and ____________________, witness, known to me to be the testator and the witnesses, respectively, whose names are signed to the attached or foregoing instrument, and, all of these persons being by me duly sworn, the testator declared to me and to the witnesses in my presence that the instrument is the testator's last will and that the testator has willingly signed or directed another to sign for him/her, and that the testator executed it as the testator's free and voluntary act for the purposes therein expressed; and each of the witnesses stated to me, in the presence of the testator, that they signed the will as witnesses and that to the best of their knowledge the testator was eighteen (18) years of age or over, of sound mind and under no constraint or undue influence.

____
Testator Signature

____
Witness Signature

____
Witness Signature

Subscribed and sworn to before me by the said testator and the said witnesses, this

____ day of _________________, 20____.

____
Notary Public

My Commission expires:

UMBRELLA INSURANCE

CONTENTS

WHAT IS AN UMBRELLA INSURANCE POLICY?

An umbrella insurance policy is extra liability insurance coverage that goes beyond the limits of the insured's homeowners, auto, or watercraft insurance. It provides an additional layer of security to those who are at risk of being sued for damages to other people's property or injuries caused to others in an accident. It also protects against libel, vandalism, slander, and invasion of privacy.

- An umbrella insurance policy is a type of personal liability coverage that goes above and beyond the amount that regular home or vehicle insurance offers.
- To own umbrella insurance, you must own standard homeowners, auto, or watercraft policy first; the umbrella policy kicks in after the regular coverage has been exhausted.
- Candidates for umbrella insurance include people who possess considerable assets or potentially hazardous things, or who engage in activities that could increase their risk of being sued.

HOW AN UMBRELLA INSURANCE POLICY WORKS

The added coverage provided by an umbrella insurance policy is most useful to high-net-worth individuals who own a lot of assets—or very expensive assets—and are at a significant risk of being sued. Small businesses also use an umbrella insurance policy to guard against potential monetary damages arising due to claims.

The premium for an umbrella insurance policy may be less expensive if the policy is purchased from the same insurer that provided the original auto, home, or watercraft insurance. Depending on the provider, the policyholder who wants to add an umbrella insurance policy is required to have a base insurance coverage of $150,000 to $250,000 for auto insurance and $250,000 to $300,000 for homeowners' insurance.

Umbrella insurance is often referred to as excess liability insurance. If a policyholder is sued for damages that exceed the liability limits of car insurance, homeowners' insurance, or other coverage types, an umbrella policy helps pay what they owe. In other words, if the dollar limit of the original policy has been exhausted, the umbrella policy acts as a fail-safe, so the insured person doesn't have to dip into savings and other assets.

Special Considerations

People who regularly purchase umbrella insurance will usually own expensive property or have significant savings. Or they may own dangerous things that can cause injury (swimming pools, trampolines, dogs, etc.). They might also engage in activities that increase their chances of lawsuits, such as:

Being a landlord

Coaching kids' sports

Serving on the board of a nonprofit

Volunteering

Regularly posting reviews of products and businesses

Participating in sports where you could easily injure others (skiing, surfing, hunting, etc.)

EXAMPLE OF AN UMBRELLA INSURANCE POLICY

To understand how umbrella insurance can help, consider the following scenario. If a driver runs a red light and accidentally hits another car, there might be significant damage to the vehicle and several people might be injured.

With car repairs totaling $50,000 and the treatment of the injuries eclipsing $500,000, the driver at fault may be liable for expenses that go far beyond the coverage limits of their insurance. An umbrella insurance policy will pick up the additional liability costs beyond the limits of car insurance coverage.

WHAT DOES A PERSONAL UMBRELLA INSURANCE POLICY COVER?

A personal umbrella policy, sometimes referred to as umbrella insurance, is meant to help protect you from large and potentially devastating liability claims or judgments. Personal umbrella coverage comes into play when your underlying liability limits (such as from a homeowners or auto insurance policy) have been reached.

WHO NEEDS UMBRELLA INSURANCE?

Umbrella insurance can benefit almost anyone. That's because accidents that result in high costs can happen to anybody. An umbrella insurance policy can help prevent you from paying out of pocket for another person's medical or legal bills if you're found responsible. For instance, suppose you are found liable after a guest is injured while swimming in your pool or playing in your yard. Or suppose you are found at fault for a car accident that injures another person. An umbrella insurance policy can help cover your resulting expenses in situations like this — up to your policy's limit.

Umbrella insurance also typically extends to other members of your household, such as your spouse, children and other relatives who live in your home and who do not have auto or property insurance in their own name. So, if your spouse causes a car accident or your teen is sued for posting a libelous comment online, your umbrella insurance policy may help protect them, as well.

Your agent can answer questions about who your policy may and may not cover.

PERSONAL UMBRELLA INSURANCE POLICY IN ACTION

Here's an example of how a personal umbrella policy works: If you're at fault in a car accident that injures another driver, your regular auto insurance may cover the other driver up to the limit you selected, say $250,000. But what happens if that limit is not enough to cover the other driver's resulting medical bills?

If the other driver's injuries are severe, you may be legally responsible for damages beyond the $250,000 your car insurance policy covers. And, if he sues you, your personal assets could be at stake. Imagine if that injured driver were a surgeon or another highly paid professional. What if the accident you caused resulted in an injury that kept him from doing his job for six months? Suddenly, he's suing you for $1 million to cover the six months he's away from work.

Your auto policy's liability coverage may pay for up to $250,000, but where would you come up with the remaining $750,000? A personal umbrella policy can help cover the additional costs when your standard insurance policy isn't enough. An umbrella policy could provide the additional coverage you need so that you don't get stuck trying to pay the remaining balance yourself. This extra policy could help protect your bank account, home and other personal property.

In most cases, personal umbrella policies are available in million-dollar increments, from $1 million to $5 million. While an umbrella policy is not required, it may offer increased protection in the unfortunate event of an accident.

WHAT IS GENERALLY NOT COVERED BY AN UMBRELLA POLICY?

YOUR PERSONAL PROPERTY

While personal umbrella insurance is designed to help cover expenses if you're held responsible for damages to someone else's property, that coverage typically won't apply if you cause damage to your own property. Suppose your bathtub overflows, destroying drywall in your home. Your own damages would be excluded from coverage. But if the overflow destroys the property of your downstairs neighbor, your personal umbrella insurance may cover the damages caused by your negligence, preventing you from paying out of pocket for the loss. It's important to note, though, that any umbrella insurance benefits would kick in only after the underlying policy limits have been exhausted.

BUSINESS LOSSES

Losses related to the operation of your business or damage to your business property would generally not be covered by a personal umbrella policy. The exclusion applies even if the business is home-based. For example, if you earn money providing day care in your home, any liabilities resulting from that arrangement would likely not be covered.

Personal umbrella insurance typically doesn't cover other business-related liabilities such as a malpractice lawsuit, or losses in connection with your paid position as an officer or member of a governing board of a for-profit organization.

CRIMINAL OR INTENTIONAL ACTIONS

A personal umbrella policy usually won't protect you from the consequences of your own intentionally harmful or illegal behavior — for example, restitution you owe if you're convicted of a crime or damage you intended to cause through your actions.

CONTRACTS

Personal umbrella insurance typically won't protect you from any liability that arises in connection with an oral or written contract you've entered. So, if you find yourself facing a lawsuit from someone you've hired to work on your home, for example, it's unlikely that your umbrella insurance would provide protection.

IS UMBRELLA INSURANCE THE SAME AS EXCESS LIABILITY INSURANCE?

Umbrella insurance is sometimes referred to as excess liability protection, but these are actually two different types of insurance.

Not all insurers offer excess liability coverage. These policies only provide coverage for the same risks as your underlying policy and come with the same exclusions. For example, if you have excess liability coverage on your homeowner's insurance policy, you'll likely have additional protection if you are found responsible for a visitor's injuries at your home. However, you probably would not have coverage for a libel or slander settlement, because defamation is not a risk covered by standard homeowner liability insurance.

Meanwhile, a personal umbrella policy typically provides greater liability coverage for situations covered by your underlying policy, as well as protection for other risks. For example, umbrella insurance can help pay for a libel or slander judgment against you, while a standard homeowners liability coverage, even if you have excess liability coverage, probably will not.

WHAT IS A SAFETY DEPOSIT BOX AND WHY DO YOU NEED ONE?

Contents

WHAT IS A SAFE DEPOSIT BOX?

A safe deposit box (or safety deposit box) is an individually secured container—usually a metal box—that stays in the safe or vault of a federally insured bank or credit union. Safe deposit boxes are used to keep valuables, important documents, and sentimental keepsakes protected. Customers rely on the security of the building and vault to safeguard their contents.

When you're looking for a place to store cash, important documents or other valuables, a safe deposit box is one option to consider. Safe deposit boxes can be an alternative to keeping a safe at home, although they may not be right in every situation. Before signing up for a safe deposit box, it's helpful to understand how they work, what they cost and when it makes sense to use one.

WHEN DID SAFETY BOXES BEGIN?

African-American inventor Henry Brown is credited with developing one of the earliest prototypes of the safe-deposit box in the United States in the late nineteenth century. Brown saw the need for a safe and convenient way to store valuable items and documents. At that time, though banks already offered a safe place to store jewelry and other material valuables, the storage was not private, and there was nothing to prevent nosy bank employees from looking through customers' personal papers. Thus, most people kept their important documents tucked away in cardboard or wooden boxes at home, unprotected from destruction and theft.

Patented on November 2, 1886, and described by its inventor as a "receptacle for storing and preserving papers," Brown's box was made of forged metal and could be sealed with a lock and key. In the decades that followed, safe-deposit boxes became a standard offering in most banks.

More Detailed Information

Procedures for renting a safe-deposit box may vary from one bank to the next, but in general you must present valid identification (such as a driver's license or passport) and complete the necessary paperwork, including a rental agreement with the bank that stipulates the monthly or annual fee, as well as various rules and regulations. When the paperwork has been signed and authorized, the bank will provide you with two keys to your safe-deposit box and will recommend that you keep them in separate locations. These are the only keys to the lock on your individual safe-deposit box. The bank does not keep its own copies, so if the keys are lost, the safe-deposit box must be drilled, and the lock replaced at your expense.

In order to access the box, you must fill out an admission request form. When the form has been approved, a bank attendant will escort you into the vault where your safe-deposit box is held. The lock on the box has two sets of tumblers requiring two keys to open it: your key and one that is held by the attendant. Neither key alone can open the box. Once the box has been unlocked, the attendant will leave you alone in a viewing room until you have finished your business and are ready to return the box to the vault.

You may authorize another person or persons (such as a spouse or a lawyer) to access your safe-deposit box, but there are strict procedures for doing so. Merely giving someone else a key will not be sufficient to grant them access.

Although rare, theft and damage to safe-deposit boxes can occur. Be advised that items kept in a safe-deposit box are not considered actual deposits to the bank (a safe-deposit box is only a storage facility provided by the bank) and are therefore not insured by the FDIC (Federal Deposit Insurance Corporation, the U.S. government agency that guarantees bank deposits). It is the responsibility of each individual safe-deposit-box holder to buy insurance for the contents of his or her box and to keep an accurate inventory of these contents at all times.

Also, it is unlawful to keep some things in a safe-deposit box, including drugs, weapons, stolen goods, and toxic, radioactive, or explosive substances. If local, state, or federal law enforcement authorities suspect that you are keeping any illegal substances in your safe-deposit box, they may obtain a warrant from the appropriate court to search and seize the contents of the box.

Recent Trends

In 2000 banks and other companies began to use technology to open up a new frontier in safe-deposit storage, offering customers electronic, or "virtual" safe-deposit boxes. This service allows customers to pay for an account in which to store their important documents (everything from legal, medical, and tax records to family photos and architectural blueprints) electronically. In order to access their account, customers must enter a user identification name or number, a PIN (personal identification number), and a password.

The benefit of electronic document storage is that customers can access their important personal information from any computer day or night, without having to visit a safe-deposit box in a bank. The service is also considered a convenient and reliable way to back up a computer hard drive. The disadvantage of such digital storage, however, is that despite extensive security measures, electronic data may still be vulnerable to certain kinds of security breaches.

What Safe Deposit Boxes Are Used For?

Safe deposit boxes can be used to store items that you may not want to keep anywhere else, including a home safe.

Having a safe deposit box could offer reassurance if you're concerned about any of your valuables being lost or stolen or documents being destroyed. For instance, if you've drafted a last Will and Testament or trust document, you may want to give a copy to your estate planning attorney and keep another copy in your safe deposit box.

The same could apply if you've drafted important contracts for a business you own. In a nutshell, safe deposit boxes are a way to ensure that your valuables are physically safe and secure in the bank's keeping.

WHAT SAFE DEPOSIT BOXES CAN (AND CAN'T) HOLD?

Safe deposit boxes can be used to store a number of items, but banks can impose guidelines on what can be kept inside them. Some of the things you might add to a safe deposit box include:

- Important papers
- Photographs
- Jewelry or watches
- Rare coins, stamps and other collectibles
- Passports or other identification documents
- Real estate deeds
- Home inventory lists
- Car title documents
- Stock certificates
- Bonds
- Gold bullion

Technically, you could keep cash in a safe deposit box, but the FDIC doesn't advise it. This mainly has to do with the limited protections extended to safe deposit boxes. But it's also important to remember that cash sitting in a box isn't earning interest the way it could if you kept it in a savings account, money market account or certificate of deposit account instead.

The kinds of things that banks typically prohibit people from storing in safe deposit boxes include:

- Firearms, ammunition or other weapons
- Explosives and/or hazardous materials
- Illegal substances, including drugs
- Alcohol
- Perishable goods
- Cremated remains

When you open a safe deposit box, the bank should present you with a lease agreement spelling out how long you'll have access to the box, what you'll pay for it and what you can or can't add to it. The lease agreement may also include a clause stating that, if the bank believes the contents of the safe deposit box are unsafe, they can force it open and dispose of whatever is inside, charging any disposal fees to you.

HOW DO SAFE DEPOSIT BOXES WORK?

When you rent a safe deposit box, the bank gives you a key to use, in tandem with a second "guard key" held by a bank employee, to access the box. If your bank uses a keyless system, you will scan your finger or hand instead. Either way, you will have to provide some type of identification—and your key, if it's not a keyless system—every time you visit the bank to access the box.

An individual can rent a box in their name only, or they can add other people to the lease. Co-lessors on a safe deposit box will have equal access and rights to the contents of the box. For example, people who have an addiction, financial, marriage, and/or judgment issues may not be ideal candidates.

Some institutions allow access to be set up so that both (or all) lessors must be present to open the safe deposit box. Experts recommend designating someone with power of attorney who can access the safe deposit box.

Safe deposit boxes are a good place to keep your hard-to-replace documents—such as contracts and business papers, military discharge papers, and physical stock and bond certificates—along with small collectibles and family heirlooms. Keep in mind that the largest safe deposit boxes are usually just 10 inches by 10 inches and two feet deep. Good things to store in your safe deposit box are important items that you won't need frequent access to, including:

- Personal papers, such as original birth certificates, adoption papers, marriage licenses, and citizenship papers.

- Copies—but not the only copies—of wills and powers of attorney.
- Military records and discharge papers.
- School transcripts and diplomas.
- Sensitive documents you would not want roommates, children, relatives, and visitors to stumble across.
- The deed to your house, along with any car titles.
- Paper stock and bond certificates (including U.S. savings bonds), if you have any (most are issued electronically these days).
- An inventory of your home's contents in case you need to file a claim with your homeowner's insurance policy.
- Important business papers and records.
- Important contracts.
- Hard drives and flash drives with backups and important data.
- Financially and/or sentimentally valuable jewelry, collectibles (such as coin or stamp collections), and family keepsakes.
- Other documents or small items that would be difficult or impossible to replace.

Safe deposit boxes can't be accessed 24/7, so it's best not to put anything in them that might be needed in a hurry.

ADVANTAGES AND DISADVANTAGES OF A SAFE DEPOSIT BOX

Safe deposit boxes are undoubtedly more secure than most people's homes. Bank vaults, of course, are harder to break into and are located in secure areas with alarms, video cameras, and top-notch locks. They're also reinforced to withstand fire, floods, hurricanes, tornadoes, and other natural disasters.

Although safe deposit boxes are designed to withstand natural disasters, it's a good idea to put anything that could be damaged by water in a waterproof container, such as a zippered plastic bag, to add another layer of protection.

It's best to store items in a safe deposit box that won't be needed in an emergency. Passports, medical directives, the only copies of wills, and powers of attorney, among other documents, are better kept in a secure spot, such as a fireproof home safe. You're better off keeping the following items out of your safe deposit box:

- Passports
- Only copies of living wills, advanced medical directives, and durable powers of attorney
- Valuables you have not insured
- Cash
- Anything illegal

The contents of a safe deposit box are not insured in the same way as a bank or credit union deposits. The Federal Deposit Insurance Corporation (FDIC) insures cash deposits up to a certain limit but, due to the fact that there is no way to verify the contents of a safe deposit box, banks will not insure their contents. Also, if heirs are not told about the location of the drawer, upon non-payment the box is considered abandoned, and its contents are turned over to the state's unclaimed-property offices for auction.

Special Considerations

Safe deposit boxes have been offered by banks for some 150 years—with various other types of safekeeping offered long before that. However, fewer people today are renting safe deposit boxes, opting instead for digital storage and home safes.

This can make it easier to find an available box—or more difficult if your bank no longer offers them. Betty Riess, a Bank of America spokeswoman, said demand for boxes has dropped "significantly," especially among younger customers who are more likely to rely on digital storage. According to Riess, fewer than half of her company's safe deposit boxes are rented.

Some banks now offer the boxes for free depending on the type of account and your balance.

CAN SAFE DEPOSIT BOXES BE SHARED WITH SOMEONE ELSE?

It's possible to open a safe deposit box with more than one person. This can be done initially when the box is leased. In that instance, all parties involved are considered co-renters.

Renters also can be added after the fact. This usually involves the new renter's visiting the bank, providing ID and signing paperwork agreeing to be added as a co-renter. In either case, co-renters would each have their own key to the box and be able to store things inside it.

Co-renters share equally in the contents of the box as well as any liability associated with the box. Sharing a safe deposit box with a spouse or someone else can be convenient if you both have an interest in what's inside it. For example, you and your spouse may decide that you want to keep copies of your wills and family heirlooms in the same place.

But that also means that any co-renter can take items out of the safe deposit box without having to okay it with other co-renters first. This could lead to problems, since the bank takes no part in settling disputes between co-renters.

Safe Deposit Box Protections

When opening a savings account, money market account or any other type of account at a bank that's FDIC insured, you enjoy certain protections. Specifically, if the bank fails, the FDIC will reimburse any money in your accounts up to federal limits.

Safe deposit boxes, on the other hand, don't work that way. Since they're not technically deposit accounts, they're not covered by FDIC rules, and banks don't have to provide any type of insurance independently. The FDIC advises banking customers that no safe deposit box is 100% protected against things like theft, fire, floods or other types of damage resulting in losses.

Since protections are limited for safe deposit boxes, banks may advise customers to take their own safety precautions. For example, that may include keeping a detailed inventory of the box's contents, along with photographs of what's inside and individually insuring valuables, such as jewelry or collectibles.

WHAT HAPPENS TO A SAFE DEPOSIT BOX IF THE OWNER DIES?

Safe deposit box lease agreements can include provisions for what happens if the person leasing the box passes away or files bankruptcy. For instance, if the person dies, the bank can allow other people to access the box if it's required to obtain necessary documents, such as a will or deeds to property. This usually requires official court documentation and may be limited to the deceased person's executor or trustee.

If the box has a surviving co-renter, the bank can temporarily block access to it from third parties until the co-renter gives their consent. The bank doesn't have to determine ownership of what's inside a safe deposit box if one renter passes away. It's important to keep in mind that how safe deposit boxes are handled when someone dies can ultimately depend on the probate laws in their state. In the case of a bankruptcy filing, the bank can allow access to the box by third parties when court documentation is provided.

HOW TO DECIDE WHEN A SAFE DEPOSIT BOX MAKES SENSE

Whether to use a safe deposit box can depend on several factors, including what you want to store in the box, the value of those items and whether they're insured in any way. Safe deposit boxes can keep your items safe, though it's important to remember that they're not foolproof.

If you're considering leasing a safe deposit box, take time to read through the terms of the lease agreement so you understand how much you're paying, what you can or can't keep in the box and what your rights and responsibilities are. You also should consider how long you want to keep the box and check the contents at least once annually if you plan to have it for more than a year.

Finally, it may be a good idea to let your family know you've opened a safe deposit box. Though you don't have to tell them what's in it, letting them know you have one is important for estate planning purposes in case something happens to you unexpectedly.

Items for Consideration

Since you may not always have immediate access to items in your safe deposit box, here is a list of items to store and items that may not be appropriate to store.

Items you should store in a safe deposit box

- *An inventory of your household possessions*. In the event of a natural disaster, you'll need that information to file a claim on your homeowner's policy.
- *Valuable jewelry or rare collectables*.
- *Stock and bond certificates and U.S. Savings bonds*. If you have paper ones, it's a good idea to store them in your safe deposit box until you're ready to utilize them.
- *Important documentation*. Consider storing paperwork such as original insurance policies, deeds, titles or mortgages.

Items you should not store in a safe deposit box

- *The only copy of your will*. In some states safe deposit boxes are sealed when the owner dies. A good piece of advice is to keep the original of your will on file at your lawyer's office.
- *Cash*. FDIC insurance doesn't cover the contents of safe deposit boxes. If you want your cash to be protected from disaster, you should deposit it in an actual bank account.
- *Anything that requires immediate access*. When you store items in a safe deposit box, keep in mind they will only be accessible during normal banking hours. If it is something you will ever need immediate access to, you're better off keeping it in a safe place at home or elsewhere.

Cover Your Assets

Though safe deposit boxes can provide a more secure option to protecting your valuables than your home, they are not immune to all disasters. Take extra precautions to protect the contents of your box. For example, it is a good idea to seal documents and other items susceptible to water damage in Ziplock bags. Furthermore, keep an inventory of the box's contents and take photos of belongings you place inside the box.

TRANSFER ON DEATH FOR BANK ACCOUNTS

Contents

WHAT IS A TOD ACCOUNT?

A transfer on death (TOD) account automatically transfers its assets to a named beneficiary when the holder dies For example, if you have a savings account with $100,000 in it and name your son as its beneficiary, that account would transfer to him upon your death.

As Fidelity Investments notes, a TOD is "a provision of a brokerage account that allows the account's assets to pass directly to an intended beneficiary; the equivalent of a beneficiary designation." Though laws governing estate planning vary by state, many bank accounts, investment accounts and even deeds are considered TOD accounts. If you own part of a TOD property, only your ownership share will transfer.

A transfer on death (TOD) account is a type of beneficiary designation that names recipient beneficiaries to receive the assets of the account at the time of the account holder's death, without the assets going through probate. You can name one or more recipients who receive the assets outright through direct distribution from your account. A payable on death (POD) account is very similar to a TOD arrangement but deals with a person's bank assets instead of their stocks, bonds, mutual funds or other investment assets.

TOD ACCOUNT BENEFICIARIES

TOD account holders can name multiple beneficiaries and divide assets any way they like. If you've opened a TOD investment account to be split evenly between your two children, each will receive half of its holdings when you die.

However, the beneficiaries have no access or rights to a TOD account while its owner is alive. Those beneficiaries can also be changed at any time, so long as the TOD account holder is deemed mentally competent. Similar to when you leave assets in a will, transfer on death doesn't establish any rights until after you die. While you live, the named beneficiaries can't access or control the accounts.

TOD Accounts vs. Wills

The most important benefit of a TOD account is simplicity.

Estate planning can help minimize the legal mess left after you die. Without it, the probate system can take over the distribution of your assets. It can also name an executor of your estate and pay off your remaining debts with your assets. It then distributes whatever is left according to your will, but only if you have one. If you don't, your assets are distributed evenly by the probate court to whatever living relatives the executor can find.

Meanwhile, when a person with a TOD account dies, the executor sends a copy of the death certificate to an agent at the account's bank or brokerage. That account is then re-registered in the beneficiary's name.

TOD Account Supersedes a Will

A TOD account skips the probate process and takes precedence over a will. If you will all of your money and property to your children but have a TOD account naming your brother the beneficiary, he will receive what's in the account and your children will get everything else.

If you have property in your will and have a TOD deed on that property, the TOD order may take precedence. The law varies by state, but banks and brokerages in many states will honor a TOD as soon as you die. If you have any doubts about a TOD contradicting your will, you may want to double-check the terms or consult an advisor.

TOD Accounts and Death

A TOD account will prevent you from compiling additional debt through probate related to executor and attorney's fees, but they can't erase your estate's debt. Creditors can still go after assets in a TOD account. TOD accounts are also subject to inheritance tax and capital gains tax, as well as taxes on withdrawals from pre-tax investments including IRAs and 401(k) plans.

TOD Accounts and Spouses

If you have a surviving spouse, investment and bank accounts will pass to them before going to a TOD account beneficiary. Depending on state law, a beneficiary may receive the assets of a TOD account only after a spouse's death, if at all. Massachusetts and Colorado are among states with strong spousal inheritance laws, so you may want to look into local law yourself or have an advisor do it for you while composing your estate plan.

WHAT ARE THE BENEFITS (PROS) OF A TRANSFER ON DEATH / PAYABLE ON DEATH ACCOUNT?

Free To Implement

Virtually every bank and financial institution offers this type of account registration, with naming of beneficiaries on an account. These accounts can be established free of charge at most institutions.

Easy To Administer

Just like naming and changing beneficiary designations on your retirement account or life insurance policy, such changes are easy to implement on TOD or POD accounts. All you need to do is complete new paperwork with the financial institution. There's no appointment with an attorney or time involved other than completing a form.

Immediate Transfer of Assets to Named Recipients

Rather than waiting for assets to pass through probate or estate administration, assets should be transferred to named beneficiaries on TOD and POD accounts within a short timeframe post submitting necessary paperwork such as a death certificate and recipient beneficiary account information.

WHAT ARE THE PITFALLS (CONS) OF A TRANSFER ON DEATH / PAY ON DEATH ACCOUNT?

While a TOD account can be divided among several beneficiaries, that doesn't mean it has to be divided equally. You may want to consult with beneficiaries and advisors to avoid any potential conflicts. Also, a TOD account with someone under 18 as a beneficiary could be an issue, as minors can't control investment accounts. If you haven't designated a guardian or set up a trust (and named a trustee), that may be a conversation worth considering.

Lack of Resources To Pay Final Expenses

Death sadly includes expenses such as paying your final bills, paying for either burial or cremation, paying your final tax payments, etc. A significant downfall with relying upon TOD or POD account registration to administer your assets upon death is that there might not be remaining assets in your estate to cover such expenses.

If there are other assets outside of your TOD or POD accounts that will remain as part of your estate or Trust, perhaps sufficient assets will be available to administer your final affairs. However, if all of your assets pass by virtue of beneficiary designation, there could be a shortfall to cover your final financial affairs.

Possible Unintended Expenses Incurred by Your Executor, Trustee or Court Appointed Representative

If the person administering your affairs is the sole recipient of your assets, then perhaps there's not a problem if he or she will assume responsibility to cover final expenses from the assets he or she receives from you.

However, if you name more than one recipient you need to consider:

- Who will bear the responsibility for your final expenses?
- Will he or she receive additional resources to help cover such expenses as compared to other named beneficiaries who won't bear such expenses?

- Will the named beneficiaries of your account(s) work together to help pay bills, even though they may not share the same legal and financial responsibilities?

If you have any hesitation about the above, an important question to ask yourself is if the person who will be responsible for your final affairs might incur unintended expenses as a result of administering your estate and final affairs.

For example, assume you have two children, and that you name each child as fifty percent beneficiaries on all of your accounts and life insurance. Assume you also name only one child as the executor of your Will and your estate. The child named as the executor legally assumes your final financial obligations, which can be significant just for cremation or burial, let alone any other expenses.

You Cannot Name an Alternate or Contingent Beneficiary

If the person you nominated to receive the proceeds dies before you, then the contents of your account are automatically transferred to your estate.

Some States Only Permit an Equal Distribution of Funds in a POD Account

As a general rule, a payable on death account can have more than one beneficiary. However, if the account holder wants each beneficiary to receive unequal portions of the assets in the account, they must check that their state laws allow it.

Other Solutions

If you have concerns about administering your assets solely by beneficiary designations, other planning solutions include:

Give an Extra Amount to the Person Responsible for Your Affairs

You could opt to allocate a larger amount to the person who will be responsible for administering your financial affairs post death. This could be achieved by virtue of allocating a larger percentage to that person or naming separate accounts to transfer to that individual.

However, an important planning note is that once assets transfer to a named beneficiary or joint account holder, the recipient might not be financially required to fulfill your final obligations. If he or she refuses to do so, court actions could be involved.

Allow Some Residual Amount to Be Included in Your Estate

Perhaps one of the easiest solutions is to allow some amount of remaining assets to be included in your estate and subject to probate. Some expenses would be incurred, but necessary resources would be available to administer your final expenses.

Establish A Revocable Trust

If you truly want to avoid probate and any public financial disclosures, while protecting the ability to administer your final affairs, consider establishing and funding a Revocable Living Trust. This instrument allows assets held in the Trust to pass free of probate while attending to your final wishes and financial provisions, as well as ultimate bequests to your loved ones.

SageVest Wealth Management counsels clients on the totality of considerations pertaining to their investment accounts and broader financial affairs. We strongly encourage consulting an attorney regarding estate planning considerations, and we frequently participate in such discussions and follow-up actions on a complimentary basis for our clients. We care about instituting the best planning techniques to achieve your needs and objectives during your lifetime, while protecting the best interests of your loved ones longer term. Please contact us with any questions about devising the most appropriate assets and planning structure for you.

CLAIMING MONEY FROM A PAYABLE-ON-DEATH BANK ACCOUNT

Learn how to claim the funds of a POD account after the death of the owner.

The owners of many bank accounts, especially savings accounts and certificates of deposit (CDs) name payable-on-death (POD) beneficiaries for the accounts. That means that when the account owner (or the last surviving owner, in the case of a joint account) dies, the POD beneficiary can simply claim the money from the bank. The deceased person's Will doesn't come into play, and there's no need for any probate court involvement, either.

The Executor's Role in Claiming POD Account Funds

When money is left to a payable-on-death beneficiary, it doesn't pass under the terms of the deceased person's will. That means the money is not part of the deceased person's probate estate, and it isn't under the control of the executor. So, if you're the executor (or administrator appointed by the court), it's not really your job to help transfer the funds to the POD beneficiary who inherits them.

Still, if the beneficiary isn't sure how to proceed, you're likely to be asked for help. And you may be in a good position to give it. If there are other accounts at the same institution, for example, you may know someone at the bank who can give helpful advice. The process shouldn't be difficult.

You may also be the one to notify POD beneficiaries that they have in fact entitled to some money. Otherwise, unless the deceased person told them, beneficiaries may not know. You'll be able to see that there's a POD beneficiary when you look at the deceased person's bank statements; just look for the term "POD" in the account name. For example, a statement might come addressed to "Florence Knight, POD Account." The POD beneficiary's name, however, may not be mentioned; you can find out who it is by contacting the bank in your capacity as personal representative of the estate.

How to Claim the Funds After Death

To collect funds in a POD bank account, all the beneficiary needs to do is go to the bank and present ID and a certified copy of the death certificate (if the bank doesn't already have one on file). The bank will have the paperwork, signed by the deceased owner, which authorized the beneficiary to inherit the funds. The beneficiary can withdraw the money or open a new account.

With a time-deposit, such as a certificate of deposit (CD), the beneficiary has a few options:

- Leave the funds in the CD until its maturation date. This would make sense if the beneficiary doesn't need the money right now and the interest rate being earned by the money is higher than what's available in other investments.
- Withdraw the funds. There is usually a penalty for withdrawing money from a CD before its maturation date, but when the CD is inherited, the new owner generally does not have to pay an early-withdrawal fee.
- Retitle the CD in the beneficiary's name. If the beneficiary wants to transfer the funds into his or her own name, the bank will probably need to rewrite the CD at whatever interest rate is currently being offered. So, if rates have gone up since the original CD was bought, this could make sense.

HOW TO TRANSFER A SAVINGS ACCOUNT AFTER DEATH

Before heirs receive assets when someone dies, such as the money in savings accounts, the ownership of those assets must be transferred. The procedure for transferring a savings account depends on how the original owner set up the account. In some cases, it's a simple process. In others, the savings account may be tied up in a lengthy probate process.

Joint Accounts

A savings account may be held jointly, and the owners have right of survivorship. Ownership of the entire account passes to the survivor or survivors on the death an owner. Typically, spouses or parents and children hold savings accounts jointly. As a surviving owner, you can withdraw money from the account. To keep everything straight, it's best to contact the bank or credit union and have the title cleared. The bank will need a certified copy of the death certificate or other proof of death.

Account Beneficiary

The sole owner of a savings account can arrange with the bank to name a beneficiary by completing a "Payable on Death" form. The named beneficiary has no claim on the account while the owner is alive. If the owner passes away, the account automatically passes to the beneficiary without the need for probate. The account beneficiary will need to provide the bank with a certified copy of the death certificate. The bank then transfers title to the account to the beneficiary.

Probated Accounts

When there is no designated beneficiary or joint owner of a savings account, it must go through probate. The probate court reviews the will and other records to determine who is entitled to get the money in the savings account. The executor of the estate, not the beneficiary, transfers ownership of the account. The probate court provides a letter authorizing the executor to act on behalf of the deceased. The executor then submits to the bank this letter, a copy of the death certificate, and either a copy of the will or a letter from the probate court stating which heir gets the savings account. The bank then processes the transfer of ownership.

POTENTIAL COMPLICATIONS

POD designations are widely used because they're simple both for the person who sets them up and the beneficiaries who inherit. Sometimes, however, circumstances can make for complications. If there's a disagreement over who inherits the funds in an account, consult a local attorney who's knowledgeable about state probate law.

Divorce

If someone names his or her spouse as a POD beneficiary, and then the couple divorces, the POD designation may—or may not—be automatically canceled. Just like the effect on the will, it depends on state law. Any former spouse who wants to claim a POD account should check the law to make sure the designation is still in effect.

Multiple Beneficiaries

It doesn't have to be a problem when more than one person is named as a POD beneficiary of a single account—commonly, the beneficiaries simply split the money evenly. Problems arise only if the beneficiaries can't agree on what to do about money tied up in a CD, or if they've inherited an asset that isn't easily divided (a large bond, for example). As always, compromise offers the best solution both for everyone's pocketbook and for long-term family relations.

Ineligible Beneficiaries

It's uncommon, but some state laws still restrict who can be named as a POD beneficiary. It's never a problem to name a natural person, but there may be prohibitions against designating a charity or other organization to inherit in this way.

Contradictory Will Provisions

What if the will leaves the account to someone other than the POD beneficiary? Almost always, the POD designation wins--it's a contract with the bank and can't be changed by will. There are exceptions, however. Some states allow people to revoke POD designations in their wills if the will specifically identifies the account. And Washington state has a "superwill" statute that lets a will override a beneficiary designation. (Wash. Rev. Code section 11.11.020.)

HOW TO AVOID COMPLICATIONS

The last thing that people want to think about while grieving the loss of a loved one is money. There are some proactive steps that you can take to help your loved ones avoid complications if you die.

"Always have a will drawn up by an estate attorney and set up beneficiary designations or TOD, but the easiest way to deal with bank accounts is to simply have an authorized signer on the account so they don't have to wait," says accountant Eric Nisall, who has recent experience with handling the accounts of a deceased loved one advises. "They can just go in and take the money or wait and remove the decedent at a later time."

If you have power of attorney for a loved one who is in poor health, you can add a joint account holder or a TOD to their accounts in preparation for the future.
Another important thing to do is to make sure that your family knows about all of your financial accounts. With the rise of online banking, it's much easier for accounts to get lost in the shuffle.

"I think a common mistake is not knowing about all of the accounts," says Nicole Rosen, a registered agent. "When my mom passed away, there was one account that didn't have a POD. I couldn't access this single bank account and it laid dormant. The bank charged enough fees to drain and overdraw the account."

So, a good strategy is to consolidate your accounts as much as possible, leaving fewer accounts for your heirs to track down.

If you're trying to find accounts left behind by a loved one, try checking your state's unclaimed money database. Banks have to surrender unused accounts to the state after a period of time set by local law. The state then lists that unclaimed money for the original owners to find before escheating it for public use. You might be able to use these databases to find money that you or your loved one forgot about.

Bottom line

No one likes to contemplate their mortality but making basic preparations with your finances can save your loved ones from financial stress while grieving your loss. Make sure to use beneficiary and POD designations whenever possible and have a will drawn up by an attorney to outline your final wishes.

TRANSFER ON DEATH FOR RETIREMENT ACCOUNTS

CONTENTS

TRANSFER OF DEATH FOR RETIREMENT ACCOUNTS

Planning is even more crucial due to the special rules associated with retirement accounts, such as IRAs and 401(k)s.

Retirement assets generally transfer directly to properly designated beneficiaries without passing through probate. However, the downside is that these assets are often subject to federal and state income tax, as well as possible federal and state estate tax. To help reduce the burden, plan properly, utilize the deduction for federal estate taxes paid on these assets, and understand the required minimum distribution (RMD) rules.

BENEFICIARY-SELECTION MISTAKES THAT CAN COST YOU

There are several ways that retirement accounts can end up in probate, however. Usually, this results from a simple misstep: messing up the beneficiary designation. Here are some examples of how that can happen.

Not Naming Your Spouse, If Necessary

In community property states—Arizona, California, Idaho, Louisiana, Nevada, New Mexico, Texas, Washington, Wisconsin, and in some cases, Alaska, South Dakota and Tennessee—a spouse is entitled to half of anything the other spouse adds to their retirement account during the marriage. That means if the retirement account owner names other beneficiaries in addition to (or instead of) their spouse, the spouse can file a claim to part of the assets; that will send the accounts to probate.

In all states, a married person must name their spouse as beneficiary to a 401(k) unless that spouse signs a special waiver.

Naming a Trust or Your Estate as Beneficiary

Any money distributed to your estate will go through probate. Bill collectors will be able to get their share before the beneficiaries of the estate get theirs.

Naming a Minor as a Beneficiary

To avoid probate, it's important to designate someone to manage the money for any beneficiaries who are still minors, until they become adults. Any financial institution can help navigate the Uniform Transfers to Minors Act.5

Forgetting to Name Alternate Beneficiaries

Designating alternate beneficiaries can keep your accounts out of probate if your primary beneficiaries have died or are otherwise unable to receive the money.

Not Keeping Beneficiaries up to Date

This all-too-common mistake can lead to some unfortunate surprises after you die. For example, an ex-spouse or former friend who is still listed as your beneficiary could receive the account's assets, rather than your current heirs.

Retirement accounts were created to provide investment vehicles for individuals so that after they have stopped working, they could access their funds to cover expenses. Accounts can be employer-sponsored, as in the case of a 401(k) plan, or they can be Individual Retirement Accounts (IRAs).

These accounts are regulated by a host of Internal Revenue Service (IRS) rules, which provide guidelines for maximum yearly contributions, penalties for early withdrawals, and mandatory distribution amounts based upon the age and life expectancy of the account holder.

When the owner of a retirement account dies, the account can be bequeathed to a beneficiary. A beneficiary can be any person or entity that the owner has chosen to receive the funds. If no beneficiary is designated beforehand, the estate will generally become the recipient of the account.

The flexibility that a beneficiary has in terms of what can be done with an inherited retirement account, as well as the tax consequences that accompany the bequest, depends on many different factors. The IRS' broad array of rules and options are based on the type of IRA (traditional or Roth), whether or not a beneficiary was designated, whether the account holder died before or after the beginning date of "required minimum distributions" (RMDs), and whether the account's sole beneficiary is a surviving spouse or widow.

Understanding the complexity of choices that face a retirement account beneficiary is key to satisfying IRS mandates, as well as maximizing the financial advantages of any inherited monies. Owners and future beneficiaries of retirement accounts are advised to seek professional advice before taking any action regarding them.

OPTIONS FOR A SURVIVING SPOUSE

A surviving spouse who is the sole beneficiary of a retirement account has several choices. According to IRS rules, he or she can:

Treat The IRA As His or Her Own

A surviving spouse can designate himself or herself as the account owner. All of the standard rules applying to the account would then apply to the surviving spouse. The spouse could then make contributions and withdrawals, and name new beneficiaries. Withdrawals are subject to a 10 percent federal income tax penalty if the spouse has not reached age 59 ½. Required minimum distributions begin at age 70 ½.

When any funds are withdrawn or distributed from the account, all nondeductible amounts would be taxable as gross income. In addition, if required minimum distributions are not taken according to IRS rules, a 50 percent excise tax is levied on the amount that was not withdrawn but should have been. (This penalty applies to all beneficiaries.)

Roll the Account Over into His or Her Own Retirement Account

Some retirement plans require that a deceased employee's account be distributed in a lump sum. In order to avert an immediate tax obligation, a surviving spouse could roll over the account into his or her own IRA or other retirement plan. (Surviving spouses have 60 days after the death to roll over the money.) Required minimum distributions would begin when the surviving spouse turns 70 ½.

Continue as the Beneficiary

This option works best if an individual dies before the age of 70 ½ and the surviving spouse has not reached 59 ½. Required distributions would be delayed until the point at which the deceased individual would have had to make them. The surviving spouse would be able to withdraw funds without incurring the 10 percent early withdrawal penalty. Once the surviving spouse reaches age 59 ½, the account could be rolled over.

A surviving spouse can also choose the 5-Year Rule option if the spouse died before age 70 ½. This election requires the surviving spouse to withdraw all of the funds by December 31 of the fifth year following the death.

If a surviving spouse is not the sole beneficiary, other rules would apply. In addition, the guidelines are different if the inherited account is a Roth IRA or another plan on which taxes have been pre-paid. Again, it's best that the plan's sponsor, a financial expert and a tax expert be consulted before any decisions are made.

Other Beneficiaries

Non-spouse beneficiaries have different options and restrictions.

They can choose:

- To cash out the account and pay taxes on the distribution.
- The 5-Year Rule payout option, if the account holder died before age 70 ½.

- To treat the account as an inherited IRA, which would require minimum distributions to be taken by December 31 of the year following the account owner's death.

Non-spouse beneficiaries cannot roll over an inherited IRA into their own account, nor can they treat the IRA as their own. In addition, non-spouse beneficiaries could be liable for paying estate taxes if the value of the retirement account plus other inherited assets exceeds estate tax exemptions.

If the beneficiary is a revocable trust, distribution rules can be extremely complex, requiring expert legal assistance.

No Designated Beneficiaries

If an account holder did not designate a beneficiary, typically the account would become part of the estate to be dispersed through probate court. If the account holder died before age 70 ½, the resulting beneficiary would be required to use the 5-Year Rule.

If the account holder died after required minimum distributions had begun, the distribution period for the beneficiary would be based on the deceased's age and distribution schedule.

The complexity of the rules for inherited retirement accounts cannot be overstated. In order to prevent a legal or financial predicament, it is imperative that an account beneficiary get reliable information from a qualified professional who is familiar with IRS regulations.

RETIREMENT TOPICS - BENEFICIARY

A beneficiary can be any person or entity the owner chooses to receive the benefits of a retirement account or an IRA after he or she dies. Beneficiaries of a retirement account or traditional IRA must include in their gross income any taxable distributions they receive.

IRA Beneficiaries

Inherited From Spouse.

If a traditional IRA is inherited from a spouse, the surviving spouse generally has the following three choices:

Treat it as his or her own IRA by designating himself or herself as the account owner.

Treat it as his or her own by rolling it over into a traditional IRA, or to the extent it is taxable, into a:

- Qualified employer plan,
- Qualified employee annuity plan (section 403(a) plan),
- Tax-sheltered annuity plan (section 403(b) plan),
- Deferred compensation plan of a state or local government (section 457(b) plan), or
- . Treat himself or herself as the beneficiary rather than treating the IRA as his or her own.

If a surviving spouse receives a distribution from his or her deceased spouse's IRA, it can be rolled over into an IRA of the surviving spouse within the 60-day time limit, as long as the distribution is not a required distribution, even if the surviving spouse is not the sole beneficiary of his or her deceased spouse's IRA.

Inherited From Someone Other Than Spouse

If the inherited traditional IRA is from anyone other than a deceased spouse, the beneficiary cannot treat it as his or her own. This means that the beneficiary cannot make any contributions to the IRA or roll over any amounts into or out of the inherited IRA. However, the beneficiary can make a trustee-to-trustee transfer as long as the IRA into which amounts are being moved is set up and maintained in the name of the deceased IRA owner for the benefit of the beneficiary.

Like the original owner, the beneficiary generally will not owe tax on the assets in the IRA until he or she receives distributions from it.

Inherited ROTH IRAs

Generally, the entire interest in a **Roth IRA** must be distributed by the end of the fifth calendar year after the year of the owner's death unless the interest is payable to a designated beneficiary over the life or life expectancy of the designated beneficiary.

If paid as an annuity, the entire interest must be payable over a period not greater than the designated beneficiary's life expectancy and distributions must begin before the end of the calendar year following the year of death. Distributions from another Roth IRA cannot be substituted for these distributions unless the other Roth IRA was inherited from the same decedent.

If the sole beneficiary is the spouse, he or she can either delay distributions until the decedent would have reached age 70½ or treat the Roth IRA as his or her own.

Beneficiaries of Qualified Plans

Generally, a beneficiary reports pension or annuity income in the same way the plan participant would have reported it. However, some special rules apply.

A beneficiary of an employee who was covered by a retirement plan can exclude from income a portion of nonperiodic distributions received that totally relieve the payer from the obligation to pay an annuity. The amount that the beneficiary can exclude is equal to the deceased employee's investment in the contract (cost).

If the beneficiary is entitled to receive a survivor annuity on the death of an employee, the beneficiary can exclude part of each annuity payment as a tax-free recovery of the employee's investment in the contract. The beneficiary must figure the tax-free part of each payment using the method that applies as if he or she were the employee.

Benefits paid to a survivor under a joint and survivor annuity must be included in the surviving spouse's gross income in the same way the retiree would have included them in gross income.

TRANSFER ON DEATH DESIGNATIONS: ADVANTAGES AND DISADVANTAGES

Whether you have a current estate plan, have an old one in need of an update, or intend to start the process tomorrow, an important consideration in implementing that plan is proper asset titling. There are various components to titling; one is using a transfer on death (TOD), generally used for investment accounts, or payable on death (POD) designation, used for bank accounts, which acts as a beneficiary designation to whom the account assets are to pass when the owner dies. Similar to naming beneficiaries on retirement accounts [IRA, 401(k), and insurance policies], accounts with TOD and POD designations are not subject to probate. For some people, it may be effective to add POD/TOD designations for a specific purpose. However, for many families, this simple way of passing assets to heirs may have unintended consequences.

This Wealth Planning Update explores some of the potential advantages and disadvantages of POD/TOD designations and pitfalls to consider.

TOD/POD Advantages*:*

- Beneficiary designations, such as POD/TOD, are simple to implement, generally have no cost associated, and allow the account to transfer to your named beneficiary relatively quickly. Upon the account owner's death, the beneficiary provides the death certificate and identification to the financial institution to receive the funds.
- Additional FDIC Insurance may be attained by having several bank accounts, each with a different title, including varying the named POD beneficiaries on each account.
- Avoidance of the probate process because the account transfers directly to the beneficiary by contract, not through a will.
- For jointly held assets, such as a home or account that is Joint Tenants with Right of Survivorship, upon one joint owner's death, the surviving joint owner will retain the asset until their death, at which time the named POD/TOD designee would receive it.

TOD/POD Disadvantages:

- If you update your estate plan and forget to update your POD/TOD beneficiaries, you may risk not achieving your wishes for your heirs.
- For any administrative costs or estate taxes due, assets that pass by TOD are not included in a pro rata portion of those expenses. For example, if one child receives your investment accounts by TOD and another child receives your residence by will, the latter may not have sufficient liquidity to pay for their pro rata share since the TOD accounts are not included in the calculation.
- During your lifetime and after death, TOD assets are legally subject to your creditors' claims. Although these accounts pass directly to the beneficiary and do not go through probate, if the executor does not have enough probate assets to pay the debts of the estate, creditors are entitled to claim some non-probate assets, including TOD accounts. While this may be difficult for creditors to do, if they have sufficient motivation, they likely will. In addition, when the beneficiary receives the assets, the assets then have no protection from a lawsuit, creditors, divorce, or other claims like they would if the assets were held in a trust.

Examples of how your plan could be inadvertently derailed with TOD designations:

♣ Tax-efficient planning

If you have a large estate (above the federal estate tax exemption amount), the tax issues can be concerning. When you have provisions in your documents to divide your estate by funding credit shelter trusts, marital trusts, and/or generation skipping trusts, passing assets outright to beneficiaries via TOD may mean that these tax planning strategies are not utilized to their full potential, resulting in an inefficient use of exemptions and possible loss of creditor protection. Even with modest estates, plans often include the ability to disclaim assets for added flexibility and the opportunity to implement a proper post-mortem plan may be beneficial to your family. However, if the accounts pass outright through a TOD provision and the heir receives benefits from the assets, the ability to properly disclaim may be lost.

♣ When you change your mind

At some point in the future, you may think differently about how you'd like to make gifts to your heirs and philanthropic causes in your community. When your goals and interests evolve, it is important to update your estate plan, and it's easy to forget about the importance of updating your asset titling as well. Therefore, if you have TOD designations, and those are not updated, your wishes may not be aligned with your estate distribution.

♣ When your circumstances change

If you have an unexpected illness or disability and you need to access the TOD account funds to cover medical bills, you may inadvertently diminish the amount those heirs were to receive or disinherit a beneficiary by exhausting the funds. Unknowingly causing some heirs to receive a greater portion of your wealth than others can add undue stress and discord to family relationships. What is the right choice for you? Your family has its own individual structure and set of values and goals, and the implementation of your estate plan needs to be coordinated in many ways, including the titling of assets. Work with your tax and legal advisors including your Wells Fargo relationship manager and Wealth Planning team, to consider your estate plan when opening new accounts or acquiring, divesting, or gifting assets. This may present opportunities to avoid potential headaches and heartaches down the road.

RULES FOR BENEFICIARIES ON RETIREMENT ACCOUNTS

A beneficiary can take out all the money from a retirement account immediately, but depending on the kind of account, may have to pay income tax on it in the year in which it's withdrawn. (This is in contrast to other money inherited from other sources, which isn't taxed as income.)

If the beneficiary doesn't need all the money right away, it can be better, from a tax standpoint, to let it stay in the retirement account for a while. For traditional retirement accounts, taxes are deferred until the money is withdrawn. (See "Tax Benefits of Retirement Plans," below.)

In most cases, a beneficiary's options depend primarily on these factors:

The kind of retirement account. Different kinds of plans—traditional IRA, Roth IRA, 401(k), and so on—are governed by different rules when it comes to taking money out after the account owner dies.

The beneficiary's relationship to the deceased person. Surviving spouses sometimes have a right to claim money in a retirement account, even if someone else was named as the beneficiary. They also have more choices, when they inherit retirement accounts funds, than do other beneficiaries.

How old the deceased person was. After age 72, people must make mandatory annual withdrawals from their traditional retirement accounts, and that affects the beneficiary as well.

How many beneficiaries were named**?** If there's more than one, special rules apply.

TAX BENEFITS OF RETIREMENT PLANS

By contributing money to a traditional IRA or 401(k) plan, it's possible to put off paying taxes until retirement, when most folks expect to be in a lower income tax bracket. The tax break comes because most contributions to these accounts are made with pretax dollars (401(k) plans) or are tax-deductible (IRAs). If the contributions grow when invested, the increase in value isn't taxed until the account owner—or, after the account owner's death, a beneficiary—withdraws the money. There's really a double benefit, because the money that would have otherwise gone to pay taxes is invested, over the years, to help grow the account.

Roth IRAs and 401(k)s operate on a different principle. Contributions are made with after-tax money, but when the money—including money from investment of the contributions—is withdrawn, it isn't subject to tax. In other words, all the growth is tax-free.

ESTATE PLANNING FOR PERSONS WITH LARGE RETIREMENT ACCOUNTS

Many of the law firm's estate planning clients in Riverside County and San Bernardino County have large retirement accounts, such as Individual Retirement Accounts (IRAs), 401-K's, and Tax-Sheltered Annuities, also known as 403(b) and 451 accounts.

Retirement Accounts Are Subject to Income Tax at Death

At the death of an owner of a large retirement account, like an IRA, the retirement asset can be subject to as many as six separate taxes. Most assets get what is known as a step-up in basis at death. What this means is that the beneficiary inherits the asset at its value at date of death and the asset can generally be sold with little or no income tax consequences. Retirement accounts are among a special class of assets known as income in respect of a decedent, or IRD. This means all retirement accounts (except for Roth IRAs) will be subject to federal income tax and state income tax at the death of the account owner. These are the first two of the six potential taxes that retirement accounts may be subject to.

Retirement Accounts May Be Subject to Estate Tax at Death

Next, if the owner's estate is large enough, the retirement asset could also be subject to a federal estate tax and a state estate tax. In 2018, a person's estate would be subject to a federal estate tax if the net estate (all assets owned by the person (including residence, retirement accounts, life insurance, stock, bonds, mutual funds, and other real estate and business interests) minus all debt of the decedent) exceeds $10,980,000. The federal estate tax is currently 40%. California does not currently impose a state estate tax, but many other states do impose state estate and inheritance taxes.

Retirement Accounts May Be Subject to Get Tax at Death

The final two taxes that could be imposed on that IRA owned by our decedent are federal and state generation-skipping transfer (GST) taxes. This tax would only be imposed if the retirement plan owner had a sufficiently large net estate, and the retirement plan owner left his or her retirement assets payable to a grandchild/other related person more than one generation younger than him or her or to an unrelated person more than thirty-seven and a half years younger.

Many of our estate planning clients desire to leave their IRAs, 401k's, and other retirement assets to grandchildren because they want to delay the income taxation of the retirement account for as long as possible. However, if the retirement plan is subject to generation-skipping transfer taxes, this would be a major mistake, as this would subject the retirement account to an additional 40% tax on top of the income taxes and estate taxes that were already paid. Because the current GST Tax exemption amount is relatively generous at $11,200,000 ($22,400,000 for a married couple with proper planning), it is relatively rare to encounter a situation where the GST Tax needs to be paid on retirement accounts. However, this will become more of a problem if the estate tax and GST Tax exemption amounts remain subject to sunset in 2024.

Retirement Accounts Are Most Heavily Taxed Assets

With all the taxes a retirement asset can be subject to at the death of the owner, it is not unusual to see the after-tax proceeds payable to the beneficiary at death suffer a shrinkage of as much as 70% – 85%. That's correct: a young beneficiary of a large IRA could be left with only 15% to 30% of the retirement account to spend after all of the tax is paid. But it doesn't have to be this way. With proper income and estate tax planning, a $1 million IRA could turn into several million in spendable after-tax cash for the beneficiary.

The Power of Tax-Deferred Compounding

Albert Einstein is quoted as saying "the most powerful force in the universe is compound interest."

Many people are unfamiliar with the power of compounding and have never heard of the Rule of 72. The Rule of 72 provides you with the answer as to how long it would take an investor at any given interest rate to double his or her money. So, at a 3% interest rate, the investor's money would double every twenty-four years. At a 7% return, the money would double in ten years. And at a 10% return, the initial investment would double in seven years.

Carrying the analysis several steps further, at a 10% return, a $1 million IRA would be worth about $4 million in fourteen years, $8 million in twenty-one years, and $16 million in twenty-eight years. In today's economy, a 10% Return seems unheard of, but historically investments such as stocks and real estate have averaged 6% to 10% annually over long investment horizons. For instance, the S & P 500 has averaged approximately 10% annually from its inception to date.

An Example of Estate Planning for A Large IRA

Let's use the example of John and Sally Smith. John is age 70 and he has an IRA of $500,000. Sally is five years younger than John. He and Sally have a comfortable lifestyle, a sizable estate, and they would like to continue to defer taxation of the IRA for as long as possible and eventually distribute it to their granddaughter, Stephanie. Let's assume for this illustration that John and Sally can invest the IRA for long term growth and that it will grow at an average return of 6% annually for the duration of the time periods illustrated.

WHY HAVING A POST OFFICE BOX IS A GOOD IDEA?

CONTENTS

A PO Box is the best choice if you have basic needs for a mailbox service that will protect your privacy or for keeping an address that you will use for mailing address purposes. In this article we'll explain the main reasons you'll want to get a PO Box.

WHAT IS A PO BOX?

A post office box, or commonly known as a PO Box or a Postal Box, is a lockable mailbox located in a post office station. PO Boxes are traditionally used to receive mail when you live in areas where mail is not delivered directly to your home. These days, PO Boxes can be used for other purposes other than necessity.

WHAT ARE THE ADVANTAGES OF A PO BOX?

The Benefits of A PO Box

Whether you run your small business from your home office or already have a dedicated storefront, you might consider a post office box, or PO Box, if you need a professional and private mailing address. Other advantages of using the United States Postal Service for a PO Box include keeping your business mail more secure, having convenient access to your mail and getting a selection of mailbox sizes and rental plan terms from which to choose.

When evaluating your business's needs, considering these benefits as well as knowing the limitations of a PO Box can help you decide whether this type of mailbox rental service works best for you.

Flexible Business Address

Having a PO Box at the post office benefits small businesses that are home-based or operate only on the internet because it provides a more **professional mailing address** than a home address does and allows you to separate business and personal mail.

If you live in a small town and want to use a more well-known town for your business address, then a PO Box provides this flexibility since you get to pick a post office in your desired location.

If you later decide to operate in a different area, you can easily forward your business mail or even transfer your PO Box for your convenience.

If you plan to use the PO Box as your official business address and have registered your business as a **corporation, limited partnership or limited liability company**, LegalZoom warns that you must **obtain a PO Box with a physical street address**. USPS offers this option at select post office locations as part of its premium PO Box services. You can visit the USPS website and use its post office locator tool to find nearby locations that offer street addressing for PO Boxes.

More Secure and Private Mail

Since the post office monitors incoming mail and your mailbox will contain a lock to **prevent unauthorized access**, a PO Box offers better security than a mailbox outside your house or building. This gives you greater peace of mind that people will not steal important letters from your mailbox or take packages left at the door. This improved security keeps your mail more private since confidential documents with your personal or business information are less likely to end up in an unauthorized person's hands.

When you receive packages that require a signature at your PO Box, there is also less risk that an unauthorized person will sign your name and accept the delivery. Instead, you can choose to have your signature on file and allow a post office representative to accept and hold the package securely until you can pick it up. This also eliminates the hassle of having to reschedule package deliveries.

Convenient Access Hours

When you're busy running your business, you may find a PO Box convenient since all your mail remains held at one place until you have a convenient time to pick it up. While some post offices just allow you to pick up your mail during their regular business hours, others offer **extended hours** in the early mornings and late evenings so that you can visit before or after work. Select locations even place the PO Boxes in a lobby location that you can conveniently access 24 hours a day for no additional fee.

Flexible Rental Options

A PO Box can offer your business more **flexible mailbox size options** than some other private mail service companies, like UPS. When choosing a PO Box size, you can consider what kinds of mail you receive and how often you plan to pick it up. You also have the option to get a smaller or larger box as your business needs change. While the number of sizes offered vary by post office location, the USPS offers these five options:

- **Extra small**: This smallest size fits up to 15 regular letters and does not accommodate more than two rolled-up magazines.
- **Small**: Similar to the extra small PO Box, this also fits up to 15 regular letters, but it is taller to accommodate up to five magazines.
- **Medium**: This option may fit businesses that receive large flat envelopes but not any boxes or other thick items.
- **Large**: This size can fit a couple small boxes along with up to 15 letters.
- **Extra-large**: You might choose this size to have enough room for several letters and parcels.

You also get the benefit of **flexible rental terms** that can work for you whether you just need the PO Box for a few months or plan to keep it for a year or longer. The USPS offers three, six and 12-month rental terms for your PO Box. The rental prices increase as the PO Box size does, and longer terms work out to a lower monthly rental cost. You can easily renew or change your rental online when the term expires.

Limitations of PO Boxes

Although PO Boxes have a lot to offer, they may not suit every small business. Unless your post office offers the street addressing option for your PO Box, you may benefit from a different private mailbox rental service, such as a UPS mailbox, if having an actual street address is important or required for your type of business. Since the major shipping providers FedEx and UPS only deliver to actual street addresses, this means you **may be limited to receiving only USPS mail** with only a PO Box number.

Depending on your post office hours and the availability of 24-hour access, you also **may have limited access to your PO Box** at times that do not fit your schedule. You may also experience inconvenience if you often receive packages that require a signature since you won't be present at the post office to personally accept such packages, although some post offices do allow you to keep your signature on file.

Getting A USPS PO Box

You can **sign up for a PO Box at the post office or via the USPS website**. When doing it online, you start the mailbox rental application process through the "Quick Tools" menu on the USPS website. The process first involves searching for the post office locations by address, zip code or city. The results will show you a list of locations, the PO Box sizes they offer, rental fees and terms and any premium PO Box services available.

To begin reserving your PO Box for your chosen location, select the box size and rental term you desire and click "Reserve Now." You can expect to log in to your USPS account and fill out an application containing the following:

- Your personal address and contact details
- Additional PO Box users you want to designate
- Optional add-on services, such as street addressing or signature on file
- Credit card payment details

After you fill in the application, you will pay a key deposit and your initial rental fee online. You will see a prompt to print the application and take it along with two forms of ID (including one photo ID like a driver's license) to your selected post office. Your post office will then assign you your PO Box number and keys.

WHAT ARE THE DISADVANTAGES OF A PO BOX?

1. **Nonprofessional address:**

If you're using your PO Box address for business it wouldn't look professional, especially when handing out to clients or when advertising your business. You also can't use this address for business registration.

2. **Only receive mail through USPS:**

PO Boxes only receive mail through USPS, not any other mail carriers like DHL, FedEx, or UPS. This can be a big disadvantage if you accept a lot of packages or shop online.

3. **It needs to be checked regularly:**

You can't let your PO Box overflow, USPS will send you notifications to update your PO Box if it keeps overflowing. And so, you need to ensure you always pick up your mail.

4. **You need to physically pick up your mail:**

Mail forwarding is quite expensive and that is why you need to regularly pick up your mail. This can get problematic if you have a busy work schedule or live far away.

WHEN IS IT IMPORTANT TO RENT A PO BOX?

Mail theft is becoming very common in the United States, especially around the holidays. A PO Box is not only a great solution for locals facing this problem but expats and travelers too that are rarely home and want to keep their mail and packages protected.

The inconvenience of a physical mailbox is needing to go pick up your mail but with a virtual PO Box, you'll be able to log into your account and view your postal mail online.

You can even send out handling requests like opening mail, forwarding packages, archiving it, deleting it, shredding or recycling it.

You can log into your PO Box through your smartphone or computer and manage your mail online. A virtual PO Box has the same advantages as a physical PO Box, only better!

When Should I Get a PO Box?

If you have simple basic needs for a mailbox service such as protecting your privacy or for keeping an address that you use for mailing address purposes, a PO Box is a smart and affordable choice.

PO Boxes, however, are not always the best choice under certain circumstances. Some reasons for why a PO Box is not ideal is for registering an LLC or corporation, which requires a physical address. Read more on why you need a business address for an LLC or corporation.

Conclusion

PO Boxes are not always the best choice if you are registering an LLC or corporation. PO Boxes are also not the most convenient mail solution if you work and travel remotely. As an alternative you might want to consider a virtual mailbox.

Virtual Post Mail provides you with a street address to receive postal mail. The unopened envelopes are scanned so you can view your mail online at your convenience. Then, you decide whether to have the mail opened and scanned, mail forwarded, or destroyed. Managing your postal mail online is so easy; you'll never want to handle mail the traditional way again.

HOW DO PO BOXES WORK?

Renting a PO Box is an easy and quick process that can get done at the Post Office or online in 3 steps. But for both cases you'll need ID verification, one must be photo ID and the second form must have your residential address.

Step #1: Pick your Post Office:

First, you need to decide on which Post Office you want to rent a PO Box in, head to the USPS website and search with your zip code or address to find the closest Post Office to you.

Be sure that your Post Office is near your home or workplace so that you can regularly stop by and pick up your mail. It is recommended to check on your PO Box at least once a week, so your mail doesn't pile up.

Step #2: Pick your PO Box size & payment plan:

There are 5 different sizes available to choose from (not all Post Offices will have all sizes available, so you need to confirm with your Post Office that they have the size you want).

The smallest size being XS which holds from 10 to 15 letters and the largest size being XL which holds flat rate boxes and packages. If you don't get a lot of mail, a small PO Box should be fine but if you like to shop online and expect packages, consider a medium or large PO Box.

As for the payment plan, you can rent a PO Box for 3 months, 6 months, or 1 year. You can rent it for 6 months that extend it to a year later if needed.

For the 6-month plan, if you cancel your subscription within the first 3 months, you'll get refunded for the last 3 months, however, if you cancel after the 3 months, you won't be refunded. Many people prefer the 6-month plan because the longer the rental time, the better the price.

For example, you could be paying $30 for the 3-month plan ($10 per month) but with the 6-month plan, you'll be paying $54, so $9 per month. And of course, the annual plan is a lower rate.

The prices vary from one location to another; the Small PO Box can reach as low as $19 with the large reaching up to $200 in some locations, for a 6-month period. Prices of a PO Box can vary depending on location, box size, and demand.

Step #3: Change of Address:

After settling on your PO Box details, you'll fill in a rental form and go to the Post Office (if you're doing it online) to receive your PO Box keys. They're a set of 2 keys; you'll be charged a $3 deposit for them.

However, if you have a premium account, they're free. When your PO Box is set, you need to apply for a change of address to start receiving mail at your PO Box. This can be done at the Post Office, or you can get it done online.

TRANSFER ON DEATH FOR DEPARTMENT OF MOTOR VEHICLES

CONTENTS

TRANSFER ON DEATH (TOD) BENEFICIARY

The owner(s) of a vehicle may create an interest in the vehicle that is transferable on death of the owner(s) by obtaining a Certificate of Title conveying the interest in the vehicle to one or more persons as transfer on death beneficiaries (each a "TOD Beneficiary").

When an owner requests to add one or more persons to the vehicle Certificate of Title as a TOD Beneficiary, the resulting title prints a statement similar to the following:

- "[Owner] transfers on death to [TOD Beneficiary];" or
- "[Owner] and [Owner] transfer on death to [TOD Beneficiary]."

A TOD Beneficiary designation that is printed on an Indiana Certificate of Title is not valid unless the vehicle owner(s) had signed the TOD statement prior to their death.

ADDING A TOD BENEFICIARY

A TOD Beneficiary may be added to an Indiana Certificate of Title at the time of purchase (title transfer), or, if you already have title to the vehicle, you may apply for new title containing the TOD designation. Bring your proof of title transfer/Certificate of Title to your local BMV license branch. Once the new title is issued containing the TOD designation, the owner must sign and date the TOD signature line on the face of the title.

TOD BENEFICIARY TAKING OWNERSHIP

A TOD Beneficiary who has acquired ownership of a vehicle, as a result of being listed on the vehicle's Indiana Certificate of Title as a TOD beneficiary, must take the Indiana title containing the TOD designation and a copy of the decedent's death certificate to a BMV license branch to apply for a new Indiana title.

Ownership of the vehicle must be transferred according to the laws and policies of the decedent's state of residence. Refer to the decedent's state of residence or visit your local BMV license branch for more information.

TRANSFER AT DEATH

DEATH WITH APPOINTMENT AS ADMINISTRATOR OR EXECUTOR

- Certificate of Title in deceased name for all vehicles 2001 and newer.
- Bill of Sales or Letter of Gift, gifts from non-immediate family members must have gift letter notarized. Immediate family members are limited to mother, father, sister, brother, son, daughter, and spouse. Complete the Affidavit of Gift of Motor Vehicles form if the vehicle is a gift.
- Original Notice of Appointment from Probate Court naming administrator/trix or executor/trix is the only acceptable document.
- Administrator/Executor signs title as seller.
- You need to complete and sign the Application for Registration.
- You need to complete and sign the Sales or Use Tax Exemption Certificate form.
- Costs are listed in the DMV Fee Table

For vehicles 2000 and older the following documents are required:

- Old Registration in Deceased's name (prior ownership required: this could be an old registration or the vehicle's title, but title is not mandatory);
- Bill of Sales or Letter of gift. Gifts from non-immediate family members must have gift letter notarized. Immediate family members are limited to mother, father, sister, brother, son, daughter, and spouse. Complete the Affidavit of Gift of Motor Vehicles form if the vehicle is a gift.
- Original "Notice of Appointment" from Probate Court naming administrator/trix or executor/trix is the only acceptable document.
- A completed and signed Application for Registration (TR-1) form.
- A completed and signed Sales Tax Form (T-334-2) form OR Sales or Use Tax Exemption Certificate (T-333-1) form.

NEXT OF KIN OR ADULT CHILDREN: NO SURVIVING SPOUSE, NO EXECUTOR

- Certificate of Title in deceased name for all vehicles 2001 and newer.

- Bill of Sales or Letter of Gift. Gifts from non-immediate family members must have gift letter notarized. Immediate family members are limited to mother, father, sister, brother, son, daughter, and spouse. Complete the Affidavit of Gift of Motor Vehicles form if the vehicle is a gift.
- You need to complete and sign the Sole Heir Affidavit form. The Heir Affidavit is the assignment or transfer. The transfer of ownership on the back of the title is left blank.
- Original Death Certificate.
- You need to complete and sign the Application for Registration.
- You need to complete and sign the Sales or Use Tax Exemption Certificate form.
- Costs are listed in the DMV Fee Table

For vehicles 2000 and older the following documents are required:

- Old Registration in Deceased's name (prior ownership required: this could be an old registration or the vehicle's title, but title is not mandatory);
- Bill of Sales or Letter of gift. Gifts from non-immediate family members must have gift letter notarized. Immediate family members are limited to mother, father, sister, brother, son, daughter, and spouse. Complete the Affidavit of Gift of Motor Vehicles form if the vehicle is a gift.
- A completed and signed Application for Registration (TR-1) form.
- A completed and signed Sales Tax Form (T-334-2) form OR Sales or Use Tax Exemption Certificate (T-333-1) form.
- A completed and signed Sole Heir Affidavit form.

PARENTS OF DECEASED: NO SURVIVING SPOUSE OR EXECUTOR

- Certificate of Title in deceased name for all vehicles 2001 and newer.
- Bill of Sales or Letter of Gift. Gifts from non-immediate family members must have gift letter notarized. Immediate family members are limited to mother, father, sister, brother, son, daughter, and spouse. Complete the Affidavit of Gift of Motor Vehicles form if the vehicle is a gift.

- Original Death Certificate.
- You need to complete and sign the Sole Heir Affidavit form. The Heir Affidavit is the assignment or transfer. Transfer of ownership on the back of the title is left blank.
- You need to complete and sign the Application for Registration.
- You need to complete and sign the Sales or Use Tax Exemption Certificate form.
- Costs are listed in the DMV Fee Table

For vehicles 2000 and older the following documents are required:

- Old Registration in Deceased's name (prior ownership required: this could be an old registration or the vehicle's title, but title is not mandatory);
- Bill of Sales or Letter of gift. Gifts from non-immediate family members must have gift letter notarized. Immediate family members are limited to mother, father, sister, brother, son, daughter, and spouse. Complete the Affidavit of Gift of Motor Vehicles form if the vehicle is a gift.
- A completed and signed Application for Registration (TR-1) form.
- A completed and signed Sales Tax Form (T-334-2) form OR Sales or Use Tax Exemption Certificate (T-333-1) form.
- A completed and signed Sole Heir Affidavit form.

NO SURVIVORS, NO EXECUTOR

- Certificate of Title in deceased name for all vehicles 2001 and newer.
- Bill of Sales or Letter of Gift. Gifts from non-immediate family members must have gift letter notarized. Immediate family members are limited to mother, father, sister, brother, son, daughter, and spouse. Complete the Affidavit of Gift of Motor Vehicles form if the vehicle is a gift.
- Original Death Certificate.
- Voluntary Executor under small estates RI General Law 33-24.1. This can be obtained at your local City or Town Hall.
- You need to complete and sign the Application for Registration.

- You need to complete and sign the Sales or Use Tax Exemption Certificate form.
- Costs are listed in the DMV Fee Table

For vehicles 2000 and older the following documents are required:

- Old Registration in Deceased's name (prior ownership required: this could be an old registration or the vehicle's title, but title is not mandatory);
- Bill of Sales or Letter of gift. Gifts from non-immediate family members must have gift letter notarized. Immediate family members are limited to mother, father, sister, brother, son, daughter, and spouse. Complete the Affidavit of Gift of Motor Vehicles form if the vehicle is a gift.
- A completed and signed Application for Registration (TR-1) form.
- A completed and signed Sales Tax Form (T-334-2) form OR Sales or Use Tax Exemption Certificate (T-333-1) form.
- Voluntary Executor under small estates RI General Law 33-24.1. This can be obtained at your local City or Town Hall.

REQUIREMENTS FOR TITLING A VEHICLE AFTER AN OWNER DIES

Once a vehicle owner has passed away, the process for transferring the car title of the deceased person varies.

For Heir

If you are an heir of a person who has died, and no personal representative has been appointed, you can transfer the title of that person's vehicle to your name by submitting a title application that is completed by the immediate heirs, who may be: the person's spouse, children, parents or siblings. You must also provide the vehicle title, an affidavit in the heirs' names, a statement from the probate court that shows no will has been probated, and a transfer of ownership. A $33 fee will apply. If you intend to sell the vehicle, it is recommended that you first obtain the title in your own name and then provide the buyer with that title, a completed affidavit signed by all immediate heirs, the probate court statement and the transfer of ownership. If you cannot locate the title to the vehicle, you will need to file a Duplicate Title Application (form MVT-8) in addition to the forms above.

For Surviving Spouse

A surviving spouse may title the vehicle in his or her name only by submitting a title application in the spouse's name (no fee is required if at the time of death, the deceased was a Maine resident and the vehicle was registered and titled in Maine), the vehicle's title, and an MVT-22 completed by the spouse. If the vehicle was financed, the spouse must submit a lien release or obtain consent from the lien holder to title in the spouse's name (form MVT-27).

If a surviving spouse sells the vehicle, the spouse should provide the buyer with the title transferred to the buyer, a release of any lien and form MVT-22 completed by the spouse. No title fee is required unless adding an additional owner. If rush service is preferred, a 10.00 rush fee will apply.

For Joint Owners (Title States "Joint Ownership")

Under the terms of "joint" ownership when a joint owner dies the surviving owner(s) retains complete ownership of the vehicle. A surviving joint owner may title the vehicle in his or her name by submitting a title application in the survivor's name, the title fee, the vehicle's title and a copy of the deceased's death certificate or form MVT-22 completed by the survivor. If the vehicle was financed, the survivor must submit a lien release or obtain consent from the lien holder to title in the survivor's name alone. (form MVT-27) If a surviving joint owner sells the vehicle, the survivor should provide the buyer with the title transferred to the buyer, a release of any lien and a copy of the deceased's death certificate or form MVT-22 completed by the survivor. If you were married to the other owner, there is no fee. If you were a joint owner with a person other than your spouse, a $33 fee will apply. This fee will also apply if you are adding an additional name to the title. If rush service is preferred, a 10.00 rush fee will apply.

For Owners in Common Other Than Spouses (There are two or more names listed on the title as owners and the title does not state joint ownership.)

In the case of common ownership, if one of the common owners dies, the surviving common owner(s) and the deceased's estate own equal shares of the vehicle. A surviving common owner may title the vehicle in his or her name by submitting a title application in the survivor's name, the title fee, the vehicle's title, form MVT-22 completed by the Personal Representative of the deceased and a transfer of ownership from the Personal Representative (a copy of the Probate Court appointment must be attached). If there is no court appointed Personal Representative, the survivor must submit a letter from Probate Court stating there is no will of the deceased's being probated and a transfer to the survivor from all immediate heirs of the deceased. In addition, any lien holder must release the lien or provide consent to title the vehicle in the survivor's name alone. (form MVT-27) If a surviving common owner sells the vehicle, the survivor must provide the buyer with all material as listed in the paragraph above except the title application and fee, as well as a transfer from the survivor to the buyer.

For Persons Purchasing a Vehicle From A Deceased Individual's Estate

A person purchasing a vehicle from an estate must obtain the title to the vehicle transferred by the Personal Representative of the estate and a copy of the Personal Representative's appointment from Probate Court. If there is no Personal Representative appointed by Probate Court, the buyer must obtain a transfer from all immediate heirs of the deceased and form MVT-22 must be signed by all immediate heirs with a statement from the court that no will is being probated.

HOW A TOD BENEFICIARY CAN CLAIM A VEHICLE

Every state has its own procedures and forms for TOD beneficiaries to follow. To find the rules in your state, start by checking the website of the motor vehicles department where the vehicle is registered. In some states, you'll find all the forms and instructions you'll need; in others, you'll need to follow up with a call to the DMV.

Generally, the TOD beneficiary will need to submit a few documents to the state DMV:

- Certificate of title to the vehicle, showing the TOD beneficiary designation
- Certified copy of the owner's death certificate, and
- Government-issued I.D.
-

If the title certificate can't be found, the beneficiary will probably have to submit a statement about the beneficiary designation. For example, in Nevada, a beneficiary who can't produce the car title must submit an affidavit (sworn statement) stating that he or she is the TOD beneficiary named on the missing title.

There is usually a small fee for issuance of a new title. The new owner will also need to re-register the car with the motor vehicles department.

POSSIBLE COMPLICATIONS

TOD designations are usually very efficient ways of transferring title to a vehicle. Sometimes, however, circumstances make things a little more complicated.

Divorce

If someone names his or her spouse as a TOD beneficiary, and then the couple divorces, the TOD designation may—or may not—be automatically canceled. It depends on state law, just like the effect of divorce on a will. Any former spouse who wants to claim a TOD vehicle should check the law to make sure the designation is still in effect.

Multiple Beneficiaries

If more than one person is named as a TOD beneficiary of a vehicle, the issues are the same ones that come up whenever two or more people inherit any tangible asset. The beneficiaries will have to decide how they want to share ownership of the vehicle: own it together, sell it and split the proceeds, or have one beneficiary buy out the other's share.

Liens on the Car

The new owner of a car takes ownership subject to any lien (legal claim) on it. For example, if the deceased owner still owed money on the car, the debt comes with the car.

Transfer on Death allows vehicle owners to add or remove a beneficiary to the title of a motor vehicle, trailer or semitrailer. The vehicle owner must be an individual, not a business. However, a business can be listed as the beneficiary.

Ownership of the vehicle passes to the beneficiary upon the death of all legal owners. The beneficiary must apply for a new title to complete the process. The new owner also must obtain a new registration in order to drive the vehicle on public streets.

Vehicles with a lienholder, lessor or titled as Tenants in Common may not carry a Transfer on Death beneficiary. A maximum of three vehicle owners and the beneficiary can be listed on a Certificate of Title.

Adding or Removing a Beneficiary

Beneficiaries may be added (or removed) by a legal owner at any time, including during other transactions such as applying for a duplicate title or when removing a lienholder or buying out a lease. Multiple vehicle owners cannot each have a different beneficiary.

The owner must submit the Certificate of Title, a Transfer on Death Application (VP 239) and a $20 Title Fee. We will mail the new title with the beneficiary listed in approximately eight weeks. It is not necessary to renew or update the vehicle registration.

All owner(s) may have to sign the Transfer on Death Application (VP 239) depending on how they are listed on the title. Owners should not sign the title itself.

- If the title says, 'person 1' AND 'person 2', all parties must sign the VP 239 form.
- If the title says, 'person 1' OR 'person 2', either party can sign without the other.

If you do not have the existing Certificate of Title, you must submit an Application for Duplicate Title and, if necessary, a Lien Release. This is for vehicles that were last titled in Nevada. If the vehicle was last titled in another state, you must obtain a duplicate title from that state and then obtain a Nevada title.

You may submit the title or other forms, the Transfer on Death Application and title fee at any DMV Full Services Office or by mail.

Transferring a Vehicle

Beneficiaries have no ownership interest in, or control of, the vehicle until after all owners have died. A beneficiary wishing to claim ownership of a vehicle must have a certified copy of the Death Certificate(s) of the owner(s).

The beneficiary must surrender the license plates. See Plate Surrender/Refunds. The deceased person's Driver License must also be surrendered to the DMV for cancellation.

The beneficiary must submit the Death Certificate(s) to the DMV along with the Certificate of Title and a $20 Title Fee. If the title is not available, a Transfer on Death - Beneficiary's Affidavit For Title (VP 241) form may be submitted in its place. An Application for Duplicate Title is not necessary. The new title will be mailed in approximately eight weeks.

You may submit the Certificate of Title or VP 241, the certified copy of the Death Certificate(s) and the Title Fee in person at any DMV Full Services Office. You may use the mail as outlined above if you are transferring the title only. If you wish to register and drive the vehicle, you must visit a DMV office.

- Transfer On Death - Beneficiary's Affidavit For Title (VP 241)
- Payment Authorization Form (ADM 205)

The beneficiary must obtain insurance and a movement permit or vehicle registration to drive the vehicle on any public street. To register the vehicle, you must obtain an emission inspection if required, pay the normal registration fees and obtain new license plates. Fee credits from the deceased person's registration do not transfer to the beneficiary.

The registered owner of a vehicle/vessel may designate a transfer on death (TOD) beneficiary to whom ownership of the vehicle/vessel may be transferred upon death of the owner. The TOD beneficiary is not a registered owner, and the signature or consent of the beneficiary is not required for any transaction involving the vehicle/vessel during the lifetime of the registered owner.

Adding a TOD Beneficiary

To add a TOD beneficiary, the following must be submitted:

- The California Certificate of Title.
- New Registered Owner section completed.

First Line—The registered owner's name is entered as usual. Only one registered owner name is permitted.

Second Line—The abbreviation "TOD" is entered followed by the beneficiary's name. Only one beneficiary name is permitted. The TOD beneficiary may be an individual, corporation, trust, partnership, association, or other entity.

Third Line—The registered owner's address is entered.

Signature Line—The registered owner's signature is required.

Line 1—The registered owner does not have to sign line 1 to add a beneficiary.

The beneficiary's signature is not required to add, change, or delete a beneficiary.

- A transfer fee to add, delete, or change a beneficiary in addition to any other fees. Refer to Appendix 1F for fees.

Changing or Revoking a TOD Beneficiary

During the lifetime of the registered owner, the owner may revoke a title held in beneficiary form or change the beneficiary's name by selling or transferring the vehicle/vessel or by submitting an application for a new title completed without a TOD beneficiary designation.

Transfer of Ownership to Beneficiary—Upon the death of the registered owner, ownership may be transferred to the TOD beneficiary.

The following must be submitted:

- The California Certificate of Title. The beneficiary must sign the name of the registered owner and countersign on line 1.
- A Statement of Facts (REG 256) form completed by the beneficiary stating the date and place of the owner's death and that they are entitled to the vehicle as the designated beneficiary.

Note: Ownership may be transferred to another person. The beneficiary must give the buyer the above documents and a bill of sale; two transfer fees are due.